Deadly Women
Volume Six
18 Shocking
True Murder Cases

Robert Keller

Please Leave Your Review of This Book At http://bit.ly/kellerbooks

ISBN- 9781090184610

© 2019 by Robert Keller

robertkellerauthor.com

All rights reserved.

No part of this publication may be copied or reproduced in any format, electronic or otherwise, without the prior, written consent of the copyright holder and publisher. This book is for informational and entertainment purposes only and the author and publisher will not be held responsible for the misuse of information contain herein, whether deliberate or incidental.

Much research, from a variety of sources, has gone into the compilation of this material. To the best knowledge of the author and publisher, the material contained herein is factually correct. Neither the publisher, nor author will be held responsible for any inaccuracies.

Table of Contents

Amber Hilberling 5
Anu Singh 11
Debra Lynn Baker 19
Ruth Snyder 27
Betty Lou Beets 35
Adelaide Bartlett 43
Susan Eubanks 51
Clara Harris 57
Laurie Dann 63
Gay Oakes 73
Inez Palmer 79
Barbara Opel 85
Eva Dugan 91
Anna Carolina Jatobá 99
Genene Jones 105
Adriana Vasco 115
Tracy Garrison 123
Deanna Laney 129

Amber Hilberling

On June 7, 2011, 19-year-old Amber Hilberling pushed her husband Josh out of the 25th story window of the University Club Tower apartment complex in Tulsa, Oklahoma. That much is indisputable. Josh fell 17 floors before his body crashed facedown into the roof of the eighth floor parking garage. Minutes later, his wife, seven months pregnant at the time, emerged screaming onto the rooftop, ran to the broken body and turned it over. She was still cradling it in her arms, crying hysterically, when the paramedics arrived. "Fix him," Amber begged them, "Oh please, fix him, fix him, fix him." But Josh Hilberling, the 23-year-old Air Force veteran, was beyond fixing. Josh Hilberling was dead. The question was: Was this a tragic accident? Or was it willful murder?

This is what Amber told the police. She said that she and Josh had been involved in an argument during which Josh had thrown a laundry basket at her. The basket had missed its intended target, instead hitting the large picture window of the apartment and cracking it. Then Josh had grabbed her and started shaking her. She'd begged him to stop but he'd ignored her. "I was pregnant and he didn't care," she told investigators. Desperate to escape, concerned for her own safety and that of her unborn child, she'd pushed out at him. Her intention was only to get him to release her, but the push caught Josh by surprise and sent him staggering backwards to collide with the already weakened window pane. As Amber watched in horror, he plunged through it and into the space beyond. It had all happened in the blink of an eye, she said.

A believable story? Perhaps. But as investigators starting comparing it to the evidence they found certain things that just didn't match up. How, for example, could the heavily pregnant Amber have mustered enough strength to push her 6-foot-6 husband with such force that he was unable to stop himself falling through the window? And why, if they'd been engaged in a furious tussle, was there no sign of a struggle inside the apartment? The answer seemed obvious to detectives. They believed that Josh Hilberling had been caught off guard, that the shove had happened when he wasn't expecting it. Further investigation provided validation for this theory. It turned out that Amber had told her grandmother a different story to the one she'd told the police. She'd admitted that she'd barged into Josh while he was hunched over and "messing with the TV."

The question was, why? Why would a recently married young woman, just months away from the birth of her first child, suddenly decide to kill her husband? And the answer to that question was not long in coming. The Hilberlings may have been married for less than a year, but the honeymoon was well and truly over. The couple had a fractious relationship, one that was plagued by domestic violence and drug abuse. Amber, who was a regular methamphetamine user, had assaulted her husband in the past, throwing a lamp at him with such force that she caused an injury which required several stitches. In the aftermath of that incident, Josh had filed for a protective order against his wife. At the same time, his parents had made a prediction that would prove chillingly accurate. They'd told their son that Amber was going to kill him unless he ended the relationship.

But Josh was no angel either. He, too, had a problem with drugs and had been released from the military because of it. And he was controlling towards Amber, forbidding her from communicating with anyone when he wasn't around and smashing her cell phone to prevent her from doing so. He'd also used violence against his young wife. One another occasion, she'd filed a complaint with the military authorities alleging that Josh had thrown a plate at her and had tried to burst one of her breast implants by squeezing her in a bear hug.

And yet, as violent as the relationship was, Amber claimed that she'd still been madly in love with Josh. She was over the moon when she found out she was pregnant with his child. Perhaps she thought that her pregnancy would facilitate a more harmonious relationship between them. It didn't, mainly because Amber continued her drug use even as her belly began to swell with the new life growing inside her.

Josh was understandably concerned over the damage this might cause to his unborn child. He was infuriated when Amber ignored his pleas to stop using. Eventually, he told his father that he was leaving Amber and would be filing for a divorce and seeking custody of the child. On the day of his death, Josh actually called his dad and asked him to pick him up at the apartment, saying that he'd finally decided to walk out on his marriage. Patrick Hilberling was at work at the time and told his son that he would collect him at the end of his shift. He never got the chance. Before the day was through, he'd received the news that every parent dreads. His beloved son had been killed, the circumstances of his death making it even more difficult to bear.

On June 8, 2011, the Tulsa Police took Amber Hilberling into custody and charged her with the murder of her husband. Amber was soon released on bond and a couple of months later gave birth to a healthy baby boy who she named Levi. But her bail would be revoked within six months, after she twice tested positive for narcotics and also, on several occasions, failed to keep her ankle bracelet tracking device charged. Those were not the only missteps she made in the lead-up to her trial.

For starters, there was the man she chose to defend her. Jasen Elias was a family friend, and his offer of help was gratefully accepted. However, Elias had never tried a criminal case before, and it was soon clear that he was out of his depth. Once that became evident, Amber's parents urged her to fire him, but Amber refused, saying that she "didn't want to hurt his feelings." That would prove to be a costly mistake. (Elias was later disbarred for several instances of misconduct, including inappropriate sexual advances towards a minor).

And then there was the plea bargain on offer. The prosecutor had proposed a sweetheart deal. Amber could plead guilty to a lesser charge and accept a term of just five years in prison. With good behavior, she'd probably have been out in three. But Amber turned it down, and her attorney did nothing to dissuade her from her reckless course of action. He allowed her to file a no-contest plea at trial, effectively throwing herself on the mercy of the court. Perhaps she thought the jurors would buy the self-defense story and would go easy on her because she was the mother of a young child. They didn't. After a trial lasting one week, the jury deliberated for just three hours before returning a guilty verdict on the charge of second-degree murder. On April 23, 2013, Amber was sentenced to 25 years behind bars.

Amber Hilberling was sent to serve her sentence at Mabel Bassett Correctional Center in McLoud, Oklahoma. She would remain there for just over three years. On October 25, 2016, Amber was found hanging by the neck from a bunk bed in her cell. Prison staff made a desperate attempt to revive her, but she was pronounced dead at the scene 15 minutes later. An autopsy would confirm that she had died from asphyxia due to hanging, in what was believed to be a suicide. That same autopsy would reveal that she'd died with methamphetamine in her system, indicating that she had continued using behind bars. It was a tragic end to a short life beset by tragedy.

Anu Singh

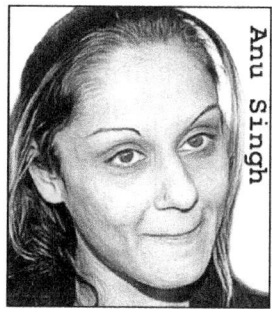

It may not have been love at first sight but there was certainly an attraction. Joe Cinque, a 26-year-old, recently qualified civil engineer had met Anu Singh, a vivacious 23-year-old law student, at a nightclub in Newcastle, Australia. He was impressed by her good looks but more so by her confident, outgoing personality. The couple got talking and soon realized that that had much in common. Both were first-generation Australians. Joe's parents had immigrated to the Commonwealth from Italy, Anu's came from India. Both Joe and Anu had excelled at school, with Joe going on to obtain his degree and Anu currently working towards hers. Both were keen on physical fitness, Joe an enthusiastic soccer player and Anu a gym fanatic. Before the evening was up, he'd asked if he could see her again and Anu had said yes.

Thus began what would quickly become an intense love affair. Joe was clearly taken with Anu and she, apparently, with him. But while Joe's feelings were pure devotion, Anu's seemed to have a slightly darker edge. Joe's friends and family soon began to notice changes to his personality. He'd always been a bubbly, outgoing kind of guy, the life of any party. Now it seemed subdued. At social events, the once gregarious young man seemed to melt into the background, allowing his girlfriend to take the limelight. And Anu demanded a lot of that light. She was outspoken and forceful, demanding always to be the center of attention. If Joe ever struck up a conversation with anyone other than her, she would appear out of the blue, to whisk him away. She also started coming between him and his family. Joe's mother, Maria, was particularly annoyed by her habit of phoning at dinner time. Joe would then abandon his meal to engage in an hour-long conversation with his girlfriend. Eventually, Maria confronted Anu and asked her to phone at 7 o'clock, rather than at six, when the family had their evening meal. Anu said that she would. Then she simply continued as before.

Such attention-seeking behavior is a well-known phenomenon to psychologists. Almost always, it marks a deeply insecure personality, and so it was with Anu Singh. Despite her intelligence and good looks, the young woman had acute issues with self-esteem. She was obsessed with her looks and her weight, desperate always for reassurance. No matter how many times Joe told her that she was beautiful, she always needed more. It was beginning to put a strain on the relationship.

But Joe wasn't about the give up on the woman he loved just yet. He figured that the solution to the problem was for him and Anu to move in together. She had since returned to Canberra to resume her law studies at Australia National University, and the long distance between them wasn't helping. Over the protests of his parents, Joe decided to give up his job and move the capital to be near Anu. Soon they'd moved into a house together, and it was then that Joe began to realize the true extent of his girlfriend's issues. She complained constantly of suffering from some or other illness. At one stage, she became convinced that she had AIDS. That turned out to be false, but still Anu remained obsessed with fad diets and with working out. She would spend hours each day at the gym and still insisted that she was overweight. "I'd rather be dead than fat," she once told a friend. And then she started displaying signs of bulimia, taking ipecac, a drug that induces vomiting.

By mid-1997, the love affair between Joe Cinque and Anu Singh was under strain, with Joe ready to cut his losses and return to Newcastle. Being part of the ongoing soap opera that was Anu's life was wearing him out. Did Anu know of Joe's plans to end the relationship? That question has never been satisfactorily answered. What we do know is that, around this time, Anu was making plans of her own, plans far more drastic than those of her boyfriend. Anu Singh was contemplating suicide, an ending worthy of the melodrama that her life had become. Not only that, but she was thinking of taking Joe Cinque with her.

Singh began planning her murder/suicide by visiting a public library and studying medical journals on ways by which a person might end their own life. The method she eventually settled on was a drug overdose, with heroin her poison of choice. Getting hold of the drug would not be a problem since she had a friend who was a user and was thus put in touch with a dealer. But Joe, who had never taken an illicit drug in his life, was hardly going to allow himself to be injected, and so Singh decided that she needed a second drug, one that could render him unconscious. Her friend and fellow law student Madhavi Rao said that she could get hold of some Rohypnol. Singh decided that it would serve her purpose perfectly.

Anu Singh's vile plan was now well founded. She was going to render her lover unconscious with Rohypnol, a medication which has gained notoriety as a date-rape drug. Then she was going to inject him with a lethal dose of heroin before applying the needle to herself. The two of them would be found dead in each other's arms, a fitting end to a tragic love affair. She was not, however, going to shuffle off into the afterlife without a proper send-off. On the night that was to be her last on earth, Anu Singh was going to stage a dinner party.

But who was to attend this bizarre rendition of the last supper? Aside from Madhavi Rao, Singh had no close friends. She therefore called on the loyal Rao to fill out the guest list for her. She had only three requirements – the guests were to be law students at the university; they were to be briefed on the purpose of the dinner; and they were not to say a word of it to Joe.

And so, on the evening of October 24, a curious occasion took place at the Canberra residence of Joe Cinque and Anu Singh. The guests were in good spirits and the food was excellent. Copious quantities of wine were consumed and conversation flowed easily. The hosts, Joe and Anu, appeared attentive and loving towards one another. Although certain dark hints were dropped between courses, no one let slip that two of those around the table would be dead by morning. As incredible though it may seem, these intelligent young people, all of them versed in the law, were involving themselves in a homicide, and not one of them was doing anything to stop it.

As it turned out, Joe and Anu would not die that night, even though it was not for lack of trying on her part. As soon as the guests had departed, she crushed several Rohypnol into a cup of coffee and offered it to Joe. In no time at all, he was unconscious and at her mercy. She then heated up the heroin in a spoon and drew it into a hypodermic. Unfortunately for her, the concoction was too thick and it congealed in the syringe. The plan had to be abandoned. Joe woke in the morning nursing a hangover from the Rohypnol. He had no idea how close he had come to death.

Anu Singh had come within a needle's breadth of killing the man she claimed to love and had been reprieved by equipment failure. To any rational person, that might have served as a wake-up call, a warning to abandon the ruinous path she was on. But not to Anu. She was soon on the phone to Madhavi Rao, instructing her to assemble a new cast of guests for another dinner party that she was hosting that same night. Then she obtained fresh supplies of heroin and Rohypnol, and the whole macabre act was played out again. This time, however, it was seen through to its conclusion. Joe Cinque was rendered unconscious and given two massive shots of heroin. Singh then sat by his bedside and watched his fitful breathing through the night. The other half of the plan, the suicide part, was quickly forgotten.

At around 12:20 on the afternoon of October 27, emergency services in Canberra received a strange call. "Could I get an ambulance, please," the female caller said. "I have a person potentially overdosed on heroin."

"Potentially overdosed?" the dispatcher asked.

"Well, he's vomiting blood everywhere," the caller said. "Is that a bad sign?"

The dispatcher then asked for her name and address, but Singh vacillated, wasting 20 valuable minutes as her demeanor alternated between cold detachment and frantic concern. When she did eventually provide her details, she gave a false name and address, further delaying the help that Joe so desperately needed. By the time paramedics were able to locate the house, the young man was in a desperate state, barely breathing and with dark spew frothing up between his lips. Within hours, he would be dead.

It did not take a genius to figure out who was responsible for Joe Cinque's death. Singh had made no secret of her intentions, and once police learned of the bizarre dinner party, she was placed under arrest and charged with murder. Also charged was Madhavi Rao, who had assisted in obtaining the drugs and arranging the party. The two women were initially scheduled to be tried together, but after their first court appearance, a judge ruled that they should have separate trials. Both of them opted to have their fate decided by a judge rather than a jury.

In the case of Anu Singh, this would prove to be a wise decision. Her counsel feared that she would not make a positive impression on a jury of his peers, and he was probably right. Singh came across as a narcissistic, self-involved young woman, an impression that was reinforced when some of her writings were read out in court. "I am a confirmed bitch," she'd written in her diary, "vain, materialistic, self-opinionated, and lascivious."

Had a jury heard those spiteful words read out in court, they might have been inclined to put Singh away for life. But the judge, persuaded by expert witnesses for the defense, saw it differently. He ruled that Singh was suffering from a personality disorder and, therefore, was not fully responsible for her actions. The murder charge was downgraded to manslaughter. Then came the sentence, which drew shouts of disgust from the victim's friends and family. For the cold-hearted murder of Joe Cinque, Anu Singh was sentenced to only 10 years in prison. Worse was to follow. The parole period was set at just four years. With time already served while awaiting trial, Singh would remain behind bars for just 18 months. Her accomplice, Madhavi Rao was acquitted of all charges.

Yet one question still remained unanswered. Why? Why would an obviously intelligent young woman commit such a senseless crime? Why would she take the life of a man who so obviously adored her? Several theories have been offered. One is that Singh knew that Joe was about to leave her and wasn't prepared to let him go. Another was that she blamed him for introducing her to ipecac, which she believed had caused damage to her health. (Cinque's family and friends deny this, saying Joe would not even have known about the medication or what it was or what it was used for.) Singh herself is no help in understanding the motive. "There's no rational motivation," she said during an interview years later. "I was mentally unwell. I still grapple with the whys."

Anu Singh was released from prison in 1999. During her incarceration, she had begun working towards a degree in criminal psychology. She would later be awarded a PhD by the University of Sydney. Her doctoral thesis was titled, *Offending Women: Toward a Greater Understanding of Women's Pathways Into and Out of Crime in Australia.*

Debra Lynn Baker

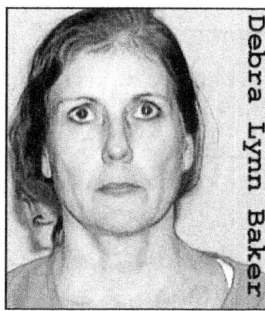

Jerry Sternadel was a self-made man. The Texan millionaire had accumulated his fortune through his plumbing business and had supplemented it considerably through one of his passions, owning and racing quarter horses. Jerry, however, was a difficult man to get along with. He did not suffer fools lightly, and he could be brusque and offhand, even to those closest to him. It was a character trait that had already cost him his first marriage.

Second wife, Lou Ann, was more resilient, apparently taking all of Jerry's barbs and bad moods on the chin and seemingly none the worse for them. There were compensations, of course, to being Mrs. Sternadel. Whatever his other flaws, Jerry was a generous man. Lou Ann, from humble beginnings, was living the high life on her husband's expansive horse ranch in Clay County, Texas.

Lou Ann Sternadel's friend, Debra Lynn Baker, had fared less well in the financial stakes, marrying her high school sweetheart, having a child, and then settling for a humdrum career as a bookkeeper.

Nothing really exciting had ever happened to her until the day that her old friend Lou Ann called her up with a job offer. Jerry Sternadel's personal bookkeeper had just quit. Would Debra be interested in the position? Of course she would! Jerry paid well, and there was a sweetener to the deal. He was offering her and her family a house on his property, just down the road from his mansion. Debra accepted almost immediately.

But Debra would soon learn that Lou Ann's caution about her husband's demanding nature had not been overstated. She was expected to be at his beck and call 24 hours a day, seven days a week. The rent-free house she'd been given turned out to be an empty benefit since she was seldom there, spending most of her time at the Sternadel estate. There, she shared an office with Lou Ann, and the two of them rejuvenated their friendship. They discovered that they still had a lot in common. They also had at least one new trait that they shared. They both hated Jerry.

To the outside world, Lou Ann Sternadel must have seemed the perfect foil for her husband's prickly disposition. She was sunshine to his storm clouds, light to his gloom. Privately, though, Lou Ann harbored plenty of animosity toward her husband. Now, at least, she had someone to talk to about it. She and Debra were often seen whispering to each other at the office, or giggling over long lunches in nearby Henrietta. So close did they appear that some began to suspect that their relationship went beyond mere friendship. If Jerry was among those who harbored suspicions, he said nothing about them to his wife or to Debra.

But in the spring of 1990, Jerry did have reason to confront his bookkeeper. The bank had returned a number of his checks, stating that there were insufficient funds. Always meticulous in his financial dealings, this had angered him greatly. And his ire had only increased when he checked the account and found that there was over $30,000 missing.

Accused of stealing, or alternately of gross incompetence, Debra had defended herself, with Lou Ann, as always, backing her up. But that had failed to placate Jerry. After reviewing the accounts himself, he discovered that it was worse than he'd first thought. Nearly $100,000 had been misappropriated over a few short months, and it was quite clear who the culprit was. Or rather the culprits (plural) because it seemed that Lou Ann was also in on the scam. That was perhaps the only thing that prevented Jerry from going directly to the authorities. Instead, he demanded repayment of the money. Failing that, he would be filing charges.

During May of 1990, Jerry Sternadel was twice rushed to the hospital with debilitating stomach cramps. On each of those occasions, he was given medication and discharged. But no amount of medicine was going to still his symptoms when he was brought in for a third time. This time, Jerry was in such agony that he was literally climbing the walls. In fact, he was thrashing around so violently that he had to be restrained by being lashed to a bed with leather straps. Doctors were mystified by his symptoms, but Jerry was quick to enlighten them. "Cut me loose!" he screamed. "I don't want to die! Those two women are killing me!"

Lou Ann was standing within earshot when Jerry made these accusations, but she shushed her husband and told the attending physicians that Jerry must be hallucinating because of the drugs he'd been given. And her theory seemed to be warranted as Jerry would later make the same accusations against hospital staff.

But whatever Jerry might have thought of the medical treatment he was being given, it appeared to work. Within days, he had recovered from the worst of his symptoms and was ready to be discharged. Over the weeks that followed, Lou Ann was the epitome of the attentive wife, catering to Jerry's every need, assisted in this endeavor by her best friend, Debra. Unfortunately, it was to no avail. On June 12, 1990, emergency services were again called to the Sternadel ranch. This time, they arrived too late.

In the aftermath of Jerry's death, Lou Ann was hardly the traditional vision of the grieving widow. She appeared in high spirits, laughing and chatting with friends at her husband's funeral. And why wouldn't she be? She stood to inherit a substantial fortune. But the smile would fade somewhat when the county coroner announced that an autopsy would be performed on Jerry Sternadel. That examination would uncover the mystery of Sternadel's unexplained illness. His body was riddled with arsenic.

So Jerry had been poisoned. The question was, by whom? The most likely suspects were his wife and bookkeeper, both of who had motive and opportunity. Debra was quite obviously concerned that Jerry would file charges of embezzlement against her over the missing money. Lou Ann, who Jerry had also accused, must have feared that he'd divorce her, leaving her destitute and quite possibly in prison alongside her best friend.

But as compelling as these motives were, the police still had to prove them, and that was more difficult than it seemed. For starters, where was the poison? How had it been obtained? Failure to place the murder weapon in the hands of the suspects was a surefire way of losing a murder case. And if either of the suspects were to be acquitted, the double jeopardy rule would apply, meaning they could never be tried again.

A year passed with no progress in the investigation, no one held accountable for Jerry Sternadel's murder. Then, in June 1992, there was an unexpected break. The lease had expired on a storage unit in Wichita Falls and, with the manager of the facility unable to contact the lessor, he was forced to break the lock. Inside were various items, including documents belonging to Jerry Sternadel. Aware of the unusual circumstances of Sternadel's death, the manager decided to call the police. When a search was carried out on the unit, it turned up a bottle of arsenic poison. Further investigation revealed that the name on the lease agreement was fictitious. The address that had been given was accurate, though. It belonged to Debra Lynn Baker.

The link that investigators had been seeking had now been established. Still, it was a year before Debra was eventually arrested on May 14, 1993. Then she was subjected to intense interrogation, much of it an attempt to implicate Lou Ann Sternadel in the crime. Despite this, Debra remained steadfast in her denials and refused to roll over on her friend. When she went on trial on January 18, 1994, she was the lone defendant in the dock.

But the prosecution case was far from watertight, with the motive it offered particularly imprecise. On the one hand, it was suggested that Debra had poisoned her employer in order to avoid prosecution for embezzlement. The jury might have bought that, but then the prosecutor muddied the waters with a secondary motive, saying that Debra had also killed Jerry because he was threatening to divorce Lou Ann, thus cutting her off from her life of luxury. Later, the defense attorney would use this theory to his client's benefit.

The defense argued that the police could provide no proof that Debra was the person who had rented the storage unit. Even if they had been able to do so, they could not prove that she'd handled the arsenic bottle, since there were no fingerprints on it. As for the claim of embezzlement, there was no evidence that Debra had taken the money. The defense claimed that someone else had done so and suggested (without naming names) that it might have been Lou Ann. As is often the case in such trials, Debra's lawyers also attacked the reputation of the victim. Jerry Sternadel was depicted as an unpleasant man who was guilty of dubious business practices and was also a serial philanderer. It was even implied that he had bedded his own stepdaughter.

In the end, the mudslinging did no good. Debra Lynn Baker was found guilty of first-degree murder. However, it was not the verdict but the sentence that attracted all the news headlines. For the callous act of slowly poisoning her employer, killing him by degrees and inflicting excruciating pain and suffering, Baker was given just 10 years' probation plus a $10,000 fine. She walked from the courtroom essentially a free woman.

In the years that followed that outrageously lenient sentence, the case has been much debated. For many observers, the jury's recommendation was predicated on one factor. They must have believed that Debra Lynn Baker had not acted alone and that her co-conspirator (and possibly the prime mover in the murder plot) had never been arrested and had never faced trial.

Whatever the case, Debra Baker would eventually end up behind bars anyway. In December 2003, she was arrested for writing bad checks, an offense that violated the conditions of her probation. She was, therefore, shipped off to the Linda Woodman State Jail in Gainesville, Texas. She would remain there until her release in 2013.

Ruth Snyder

It was the classic love triangle: the uncaring husband, the neglected wife and the henpecked lover. Only in this case, the sordid affair would end in death for all three of the players, one to murder, the other two to the electric chair.

Albert Schneider was an energetic young man with a love of sailing, fishing, and bowling. He was also successful, the art editor of Motor Boating magazine at the age of just 32. But not everything in Albert's life was harmonious. A few years earlier he'd lost his fiancée, Jesse Guishard, to pneumonia. Albert had been at Jesse's bedside when she'd died. Her death had left him deeply affected, and he'd found solace in his work, displaying a drive that made him, at times, impatient and irritable.

One day, Albert was talking to a manufacturer on the phone when the exchange dropped the call. Annoyed, he called the telephone operator and unleashed an angry flurry of words. Later, having regained his composure, he decided that he'd overstepped the mark.

The operator had been obviously upset by his outburst but had been polite and apologetic. This had impressed Albert, and he decided that he wanted to apologize to her in person. He found out where she worked and, hours later, stood face to face with a pretty 19-year-old named Ruth Brown.

Albert was instantly captivated by the blonde, blue-eyed Ruth. It wasn't long before the two of them were dating. When Albert eventually proposed marriage, Ruth accepted. He even agreed to change his name from Schneider to the less Germanic Snyder.

The Snyders' marriage was not a happy one. Right from the start, there were problems. Ruth was vivacious and outgoing. She enjoyed parties and dancing. Albert, on the other hand, loved sports and the outdoors, and when not engaged in those activities, he enjoyed art and reading. He longed for a companion with whom he could discuss culture and politics and share ideas. Ruth was not that person.

To make matters worse, Albert was still obsessed with his dead fiancée. He wore a necktie pin with the initials J.G., and his sailboat was named the 'Jesse G'. Worse still, the couple's living room was decorated with a large framed photograph of Jesse. Ruth wanted it taken down. Albert stoutly refused.

A further wedge was driven between the couple when Ruth fell pregnant. She thought that Albert would be delighted at the news, but instead, he was annoyed. When their daughter, Lorraine, was born, he distanced himself from any parental responsibility. He also complained that childbirth had ruined his wife's figure.

By 1923, the family was living in Queens Village, Long Island, with Ruth's mother, Josephine Brown, also in residence. Having a ready babysitter at hand allowed the extrovert Ruth the chance to spread her wings, and she grasped the opportunity with both hands. She began attending parties and socials and, according to some accounts, picking up men who she accompanied to various hotels for sex.

One day, in June 1925, Ruth was lunching with a friend at a Manhattan restaurant when she was introduced to Judd Gray, a diminutive, bespectacled man who made his living as a corset salesman. Gray was 33 years old and married at the time. He was a dapper dresser with a preference for tight-fitting three-piece suits, spats, and Homburg hats. It wasn't long before he and Ruth had become lovers.

The couple began meeting clandestinely at a number of Manhattan hotels, most commonly the Waldorf Astoria. On a number of occasions, Lorraine Snyder accompanied Ruth and was left in the foyer, while her mother and Judd Gray carried on their tawdry affair upstairs. Ruth was the dominant partner in the relationship. She referred to Judd as "Lover Boy," or "Budd" while the hen-pecked Judd referred to her as "Momsie."

But it wasn't long before the secret affair was no longer enough for Ruth Snyder. She began to covet a future with Judd. And that meant that she needed Albert out of the way.

In late 1925, Ruth insured Albert's life for $100,000. Thereafter, she made at least seven unsuccessful attempts to rid herself of him. These included poisoning, drowning, by "accidentally" pushing him from his boat, and crushing him under his car by pushing the jack away while he was working on it. For his part, Albert appears to have been oblivious to his wife's assassination attempts. He blamed them on her clumsiness.

Inevitably, Snyder turned to Gray to assist her in killing her husband. He refused outright, but Ruth wasn't giving in that easily. She cajoled, pleaded and finally threatened Gray with ending the relationship. Faced with that prospect, he eventually agreed.

The date of the murder was set for March 19, 1927. On that day, Judd Gray worked in Syracuse, New York, before taking the train to Long Island, arriving in the early evening. He'd been drinking heavily and wandered the streets chugging from an open bottle of bootleg whiskey, perhaps hoping to be arrested and thereby relieved of his promise to Ruth. He wasn't.

Albert and Ruth, meanwhile, were attending a party at a neighbor's house. When Judd Gray arrived at their home, he entered through a back door that Ruth had left open for him, then walked to a spare room where Ruth had laid out the implements of murder: a bottle of chloroform, an iron sash weight, and a length of picture wire.

Gray sat down on the floor and continued drinking. Eventually, he heard the Snyders returning. At around 2 a.m., the door to the spare room opened and Ruth entered the room, dressed only in a slip. While Albert Snyder lay sleeping downstairs, the two of them made love on the floor. Then Ruth led Judd downstairs to the master bedroom.

According to the plan, Gray was to enter the room and bludgeon Albert Snyder to death as he slept. But the blow he delivered was tentative and weak. Albert sat up in bed, shouting in pain. The terrified Gray called out, "Momsie, Momsie, for God's sake, help!"

Ruth had been standing in the hallway, but at the sound of her lover's cry, she rushed in, grabbed the weight from Gray and crashed it down on Albert's head, knocking him unconscious. She then twisted the picture wire around Albert's throat, winding it so tightly that it cut into the skin. Then she ordered Gray to place a chloroform-soaked rag over Albert's face. Gray was shaking so badly that he spilled the liquid, causing burns to the victim's flesh.

Some five hours later, at around 7:30 a.m., Ruth Snyder appeared in her daughter's bedroom. She was bound and gagged, but she managed to nudge the child awake. Then, after the gag was removed, she told Lorraine to go to the neighbors and call the police. This the child did, but after making the call, the neighbors arrived at the Snyder house. They tried to untie Ruth, but she forbade it. She wanted the police to find her tied up.

When the police arrived on the scene, they were immediately suspicious of Ruth Snyder. For starters, the ropes around her wrists were so loose that she could have easily escaped. Why hadn't she? Then, the story she told, about an 'Italian-looking' burglar wearing a false mustache, was utterly ludicrous. An Italian newspaper left at the scene in order to support her story also aroused suspicion.

A search of the house, however, produced more viable clues. Jewelry that Ruth claimed had been taken in the robbery was found hidden under a mattress. Then the murder weapon was found, concealed in a toolbox in the basement, and Ruth's telephone book turned up the name and number of Judd Gray, heavily circled in red ink. The police picked Gray up for questioning, and it didn't take long before he cracked.

When Ruth Snyder was confronted with Gray's confession, her response was typical. "Poor Judd," she said. "I promised not to tell." She went on to paint Gray as a man obsessed, who'd murdered her husband so that he could be with her. According to her version of events, she'd had nothing to do with the murder.

Ruth Snyder and Judd Gray went on trial in Queens County on April 27, 1927. The pair had separate counsel and, from the outset, each tried to portray themselves as the innocent party in the whole affair. The trial was a sensation, drawing huge crowds, massive press coverage, and even a number of New York luminaries to the proceedings.

In the end, there was only ever likely to be one outcome. On May 9, 1927, a jury deliberated for just ninety minutes before pronouncing them both guilty. The 'Granite Woman' and the 'Putty Man', as the press had dubbed them, were sentenced to die in the electric chair.

Ruth Snyder and Judd Gray were taken to the Death House at Sing Sing to await execution. Shortly after her arrival, Snyder converted to Catholicism in what many saw as a cynical attempt to win a reprieve from New York's Roman Catholic Governor, Alfred Smith. If that was the intention, it didn't work.

On January 12, 1928, the murderers of Albert Snyder were put to death. Ruth went first, a bald spot shaved on her head so that the electrodes could be attached. She had to be carried to the chair and started screaming the moment she was placed in it. Then she went limp and started muttering incoherently.

"Father, forgive them, they know not what they do," she said as the black leather mask was placed over her face. Then the electrical current was passed through her body, ending her life.

As the execution was taking place, Thomas Howard, a journalist from the New York Daily News, raised his trouser cuff and snapped a picture using a camera he'd hidden there. That illegally taken picture would feature on the front page of the paper the following day and would guarantee lasting infamy for Ruth Snyder.

Judd Gray's death was somewhat less melodramatic. He walked to the chair under his own steam and prayed with a clergyman as he was strapped in and the preparations were made. Then the Putty Man received a jolt of electricity. He was declared dead soon after.

Betty Lou Beets

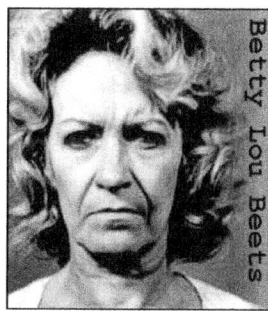

Jimmy Don Beets had once been a captain with the Dallas Fire Department. Now, though, he was enjoying a well-deserved retirement, living with his wife, Betty Lou, in a double-wide trailer in Gun Barrel City, Texas. Despite suffering from a heart condition, for which he took prescription medication, Jimmy Don remained active in his sixties. He was particularly fond of fishing and would often take his boat out on Cedar Creek Lake, a popular getaway for residents of nearby Dallas. There, he'd happily wile away the hours, dangling a line in the water and enjoying the time alone.

On August 6, 1983, Jimmy set off on one of his fishing trips and never returned. That evening, his wife placed a desperate call to the police, saying that he had gone out on the water that day and adding that he had a heart condition. A search was then launched, focusing on the lake and involving deputies from the Henderson County Sheriff's office and agents of the Texas Parks and Wildlife Department. There were also volunteers from every fire department in the area. Jimmy Don was a much-respected colleague.

But despite the best efforts of the searchers, despite the long hours spent dragging the lake and combing its three artificial islands and the surrounding pine and oak forests, there was no clue as to Jimmy Don's fate. Then, on August 12, there was finally a break, albeit not a promising one. Jimmy Don's boat was found drifting near the Redwood Beach Marina. Inside were Jimmy's eyeglasses, his fishing license, his nitroglycerine tablets, and a life jacket. Of Jimmy, though, there was no trace. The consensus, at this time, was that he'd fallen overboard and drowned. Eventually, the search was called off.

Betty Lou Beets appeared distraught over her husband's disappearance, and who could blame her? When it came to relationships, her life's story looked like the lyric sheet of a country song. Married for the first time at 15, Betty Lou would remain with Robert Branson for 17 years, giving him six children before Branson broke her heart by leaving her for another woman. She next married a man named Billy Lane, but that marriage was marred by domestic violence. It was over when Betty shot Bill in the back during an argument. She was initially charged with attempted murder, although that was reduced to aggravated assault after Billy testified that Betty had been defending herself. The couple would later remarry, although it lasted only a month the second time around.

Six years after her divorce from Billy Lane, Betty Lou married her third husband, Ronnie Threlkold. The couple moved to Little Rock, Arkansas, but the marriage soon picked up the pattern of the previous one. Betty was insanely jealous of Ronnie and accused him of sleeping with everyone, including her grown daughters. On one occasion, she came after him with a tire iron. Another time, she tried to run him over with her car. Eventually, Ronnie decided that he'd had enough and walked out. Less than a year later, Betty tied the knot with Doyle Wayne Baker.

But a change of husband did not bring about a change of fortunes. Soon the whole pattern repeated itself. The couple separated, then reconciled, then divorced, then remarried. They settled eventually in Gun Barrel City, where Betty bought a half-acre lot by the lake and Doyle paid for a trailer to put on it. For a time, it seemed that they had finally put their troubles behind them, but then, one night in October 1981, Doyle was gone. According to Betty's tearful explanation, her husband had deserted her. Curiously, though, he'd told none of his friends, nor his employer, that he planned on leaving town.

And now, another of Betty Lou's husbands was missing, and not everyone was buying the grieving widow act. It did not go unnoticed that, despite her apparent distress, Betty Lou had wasted little time in contacting the insurance company regarding her payout. She was enraged to learn that there would be no payment without a death certificate and that it would take seven years before her husband could be declared legally dead. She'd then taken to pestering the Dallas Fire Department over Jimmy's $1,200-a-month pension which she felt should now accrue to her. She also became involved in a bitter dispute with Jimmy Don's son, Jamie, over the proceeds of her husband's estate. Eventually, the estate would have to obtain a restraining order against her to prevent her illegally selling off assets.

Meanwhile, the police were also flummoxed over the lack of a body. Drowning victims seldom remain underwater. Their bodies are usually pushed to the surface once postmortem gases build up. Yet this hadn't happened with Jimmy Don Beets, and that just didn't seem right. Had the corpse become snagged on something under the water? Was he in the water at all? Had he met with foul play? There was no way to answer those questions and no way to validate the suspicions of investigators. As far as the world knew, Jimmy Beets was the victim of a tragic drowning accident.

Two years passed, during which the disappearance of Jimmy Don Beets remained an unfathomable mystery. Then, in March of 1985, there was an unexpected break in the case. That was when a jailhouse informant contacted Henderson County Sheriff's Deputy Rick Rose and offered information in exchange for a reduced sentence. He said that a friend of his had picked up Betty Lou Beets for a one-night stand shortly after her husband's death. During their sexual encounter, a highly intoxicated Betty Lou had confided that she'd killed her husband and that her son had helped her dispose of the remains, which they'd buried in the garden.

Rose was initially skeptical of this tip-off, but he nonetheless tracked down Betty Lou's son and brought him in for questioning. Robert Branson Jr. quickly cracked under interrogation, admitting that the tip-off Rose had received was accurate. According to him, the murder was committed on August 5, 1983. That was the night that his mother told him to leave the trailer for a few hours, nonchalantly informing him, "I'm going to kill Jimmy Don." Robby was shocked by this pronouncement. He liked Jimmy Don, who had always treated him, his mother, and his siblings with love and respect. Still, he did what he was told, leaving the house and taking his younger brother with him. His mother had told him to stay away for several hours, and he followed that instruction to the letter. When he eventually returned, his mother told him that she'd shot Jimmy Don in the head and in the chest while he was sleeping. Now the body was laid out on the bedroom floor, encased in a blue sleeping bag. Betty Lou, slight of frame, was unable to move it, so she instructed Robby to help her. Together, they dragged Jimmy Don out into the garden and buried him under an ornamental wishing well. Jimmy Don had recently built that fixture, at the behest of his wife.

With the body disposed of, Betty Lou instructed Robby to help her stage her husband's disappearance. After they towed Jimmy's boat down to the lakeshore, she carefully placed the fishing license, pills, glasses, and life jacket. Then she and Robby pushed the boat out into the water, pointing it towards a secluded part of the lake to delay discovery. But for the unanticipated seven-year wait for a payout, Betty Lou Beets must have thought that she'd committed the perfect crime.

In June 1985, the police finally had a warrant to carry out a search at Betty Lou's trailer. Before they could serve it, there was another twist in the plot. The property was destroyed in a fire, later determined to be arson. Still, that didn't prevent investigators from evacuating the makeshift grave under the wishing well and recovering Jimmy Don Beets's body, exactly where Robby had said it would be. Aside from that, they also recovered nineteen guns, including the .38 that would turn out to be the murder weapon. And then, there was an entirely unexpected discovery. Searching the ruins of a destroyed shed, officers found a second grave, this one containing the mortal remains of Doyle Wayne Barker, the husband who had supposedly abandoned Betty Lou four years earlier. He'd been shot three times in the head.

Brought to trial for the murder of Jimmy Don Beets, Betty Lou employed a defense that was almost as heinous as the murders she had committed – she tried to pin the killing on her son. According to her, Jimmy Don had been drunk, and he and Robby had gotten into a fight. She'd heard a shot from the bedroom and had rushed in to find Jimmy

Don dead and Robby holding the gun. She had then agreed to help Robby dispose of the body. She also claimed that she'd had no idea that Doyle Wayne Barker was buried on the property and did not know who had killed him.

Unfortunately for Betty Lou, the evidence did not support her story. Both victims had been shot with the same weapon – her weapon. She had also told lies about Doyle Barker's disappearance, saying that he'd walked out on her. Additionally, experts testified that the wounds the men had suffered could not have been inflicted during a fight. They had been shot while they were incapacitated. In the end, the jury had an easy decision to make.

Betty Lou Beets was convicted of first-degree murder and sentenced to death. On death row in Huntsville Texas, she was cellmates with some of the state's most notorious female murderers, including Karla Faye Tucker and Darlie Routier. Like Tucker, she became a born-again Christian behind bars. She also came up with a new strategy to fuel her appeals. She was now claiming that she was a battered woman and had been suffering from Post-Traumatic Stress Disorder at the time that she'd shot Jimmy Beets.

It is easy to dismiss these claims as opportunistic. Both Battered Woman Syndrome and PTSD had been much in the news while Betty Lou was on death row, with a number of acquittals in high profile cases. And there is definitely evidence to suggest that Betty Lou suffered physical and sexual abuse at the hands of at least one of her husbands, Billy Lane.

But there was no abuse inflicted by Jimmy Don Beets; even Betty Lou's own children admitted that. According to them, Jimmy was a loving and devoted husband who doted on his wife. She repaid him by shooting him in the head while he slept in order to cash in on his life insurance.

Betty Lou Beets was put to death by lethal injection on February 24, 2000, becoming the fourth US woman to be judicially executed since the reinstatement of the death penalty. In the run-up to her execution, she had received considerable support from anti-capital punishment campaigners who put pressure on Texas Governor George W. Bush to commute the sentence. Bush refused and the execution went ahead. "What my husbands started, the state of Texas will finish," Beets said in an interview shortly before her death. No doubt, the families of Doyle Wayne Barker and Jimmy Don Beets hold a different view on the issue.

Adelaide Bartlett

On the surface, it seemed like a good match. Adelaide de la Tremoille was 19 years old and pretty. She was, however, an orphan with no means of support. Thomas Edwin Bartlett was 29, a grocer, and possessed of a considerable fortune. He might have been a good catch for a young girl, but Bartlett wasn't in the best of health. His rotting teeth gave him nasty halitosis, and he was afflicted with several ailments, including tapeworm. He was also somewhat of a hypochondriac with a particular interest in quack medicines and the paranormal.

These impediments notwithstanding, Adelaide appears to have been genuinely fond of Edwin. She was also not about to turn down the chance of financial security. When Edwin proposed, she gleefully said yes. The couple was married in 1875. Thereafter, they set up home in the London suburb of Herne Hill, and Adelaide fulfilled her ambition of furthering her studies, with her husband footing the bill.

Six years into the marriage, in 1881, Adelaide was pregnant with her first child. The baby, however, was stillborn. Thereafter, Edwin insisted that they would henceforth have a platonic relationship. According to Adelaide's later testimony, he gave her permission to service her sexual needs elsewhere. It was also around this time that he made a will, leaving his entire estate to Adelaide, on the condition that she did not remarry after his death.

Enter into the picture the Rev. George Dyson, a pale, serious-looking clergyman who served the Wesleyan congregation in Merton Abbey. The Bartletts started attending his sermons in January 1885, and a friendship was soon struck between them and the preacher. Dyson was an educated man with a BA degree from Dublin University. Edwin soon suggested that he might assist Adelaide in her studies. Thereafter, Dyson became a regular visitor to the Bartlett residence. When the couple moved to the upscale London suburb of Pimlico in the autumn of that year, Edwin went so far as to buy the vicar a season railway ticket, so that he could visit them often. This he did. Before long, he and Adelaide Bartlett were engaged in a sexual relationship.

By now, Edwin was beginning to suffer from severe health problems. His decaying teeth were causing him untold agony and were poisoning his system. The pain made it impossible for him to sleep at night, and he existed in a daze due to insomnia. A doctor regularly attended him and on December 29, 1885, told Adelaide that he feared that necrosis, or cell death, might set in.

Two days later, at around 4 o'clock on the morning of the New Year, the Bartletts' landlord was awakened by a loud banging on his front door. The bleary-eyed man opened up to find an obviously agitated

Adelaide Bartlett on his doorstep. "Come quickly!" she cried. "Mr. Bartlett is dead!"

Edwin Bartlett had indeed passed away during the night and, given his state of health, no one was really surprised. No one, that is, but Edwin's father. The old man had never liked Adelaide and had often accused her of infidelity. He'd even suggested, during the early years of her marriage to Edwin, that she'd been sleeping with Edwin's younger brother. Now he was making a far more serious allegation. He was accusing Adelaide of murder. According to Dyson senior, he had detected a strong whiff of chloroform when he'd visited Edwin's corpse and leaned in to kiss his son on the lips.

An autopsy was thus ordered and carried out on January 7, 1886. The results were surprising. Edwin, for all of his supposed frailty, had actually been in fairly good health. There was, however, an overwhelming smell of chloroform when the doctors opened the stomach, suggesting that he'd ingested a quantity of that substance. What the coroner couldn't figure out was how. Chloroform is highly corrosive and, if swallowed, usually causes burns to the mouth, throat, and larynx. Yet Bartlett displayed none of these injuries. It was a perplexing problem, but not so perplexing that it deflected the coroner from his conclusion. Cause of death was poisoning by chloroform. Edwin Bartlett had been murdered.

The obvious suspect was the supposedly grieving Adelaide, and she was soon arrested. Then, after the police learned of her close relationship with Rev. Dyson, he, too, was brought in for questioning. Under interrogation, they told different stories. Adelaide admitted that she'd been sleeping with the vicar but claimed that her husband knew of the relationship and had even encouraged it. Dyson denied any impropriety but confessed to obtaining the chloroform for Mrs. Bartlett, albeit under false pretenses.

According to Dyson, Adelaide had approached him on December 27 and asked him to buy some chloroform for her. She'd said that she used it as a sedative for her husband, as it was the only way that he was able to get any sleep. Dyson had complied with the request, but his method of obtaining the chloroform would later raise suspicion. Rather than buying the substance from a single pharmacy and signing the Poisons Register (as was required by law), he'd visited four different druggists and obtained small quantities which fell under the legal requirement for reporting. He'd also lied about the purpose of his purchases, saying that he needed the chloroform to remove stains from his clothing. All in all, he acquired four ounces, which he poured into a single bottle. This he handed to Adelaide Bartlett.

After hearing that there was to be an autopsy, Dyson said that he had contacted Adelaide and asked what she had done with the chloroform. She'd assured him that she had never used it and still had the full bottle. However, she later told him that she had thrown the container and its contents away, tossing it from a railway carriage. When Dyson said that he might have to inform the authorities that he'd bought the chloroform for her, Adelaide had coyly informed him, "If you don't incriminate me, I won't incriminate you." That was what had convinced him to come forward and tell what he knew.

Dyson would later repeat this story, almost verbatim, to the Coroner's jury. But his evidence came across as self-serving and contrived at the inquest. In any case, it did not impress the jury. It returned an indictment of willful murder against Adelaide Bartlett and accessory before the fact against Dyson.

The trial of Bartlett and Dyson got underway on April 12, 1886, at London's Old Bailey. The murder had attracted massive press coverage, both in the UK and abroad, and that was reflected in the huge crowds that gathered outside the courtroom, all hoping for a seat in the gallery. For George Dyson, the ordeal would soon be over. The charge sheet had just been read when the prosecution asked for the charges against Dyson to be dropped. They intended calling him as a witness against Adelaide Bartlett instead.

Fortunately for Adelaide, she had a hugely competent defender in Sir Edward Clarke, considered the finest barrister in England at the time. The defense that he came up with was a masterstroke. He contended that Edwin Bartlett had committed suicide.

Clarke's theory was based on the anomaly in the autopsy results – the lack of chloroform burns in the victim's mouth, throat, and larynx. According to him, this could only be the case if Bartlett had downed the chloroform in a single gulp. Had the liquid been forced on him, he would undoubtedly have tried to spit it out, causing the telltale burns. Clarke also made short work of the prosecution's two key witnesses. He portrayed Bartlett senior as bitter and motivated by money, wanting to keep his son's estate for himself rather than allowing it to go to his daughter-in-law. As for Rev. Dyson, Clarke said he was a jilted lover who resented the fact that Adelaide, whatever her indiscretions, truly loved her husband. Clarke even got the examining physician to admit on the stand that suicide was a possibility.

But there was one piece of evidence that weighed strongly against the suicide theory. On the last evening of his life, Edwin Bartlett had instructed his cook to prepare a sumptuous meal for New Year's Day – hardly the act one would expect of a man contemplating suicide. The prosecution also offered a possible motive for the murder, suggesting that Edwin had recently told his wife that he wanted to resume their physical relationship. She, repulsed by him and in love with Rev. Dyson, had decided she'd rather commit murder than submit.

Adelaide Bartlett did not testify in her own defense, since the law of England forbade it at the time (the Criminal Evidence Act would be amended a decade later in 1898). Sir Edward Clarke, in fact, called no witnesses at all. He did, however, deliver an impassioned six-hour closing argument on behalf of his client. That, in the end, was enough to sway the jury. "Although we think grave suspicion is attached to the prisoner," the foreman informed the court, "we do not think there is sufficient evidence to show how or by whom the chloroform was administered. We therefore find Adelaide Bartlett not guilty of murder."

The not guilty verdict was greeted by rapturous applause from the gallery. Adelaide Bartlett had clearly won the hearts of the public, although many believed that she'd gotten away with murder. As the renowned surgeon, Sir James Paget, famously quipped: "Now that she has been acquitted of murder and cannot be tried again, she should tell us, in the interests of science, how she did it."

Adelaide Bartlett disappeared from public life after her infamous trial. Her fate remains unknown, although it has been suggested that she immigrated to the United States, settled in Connecticut, and died there in 1933. There are also conflicting reports as to what happened to the Rev. Dyson. One version has him immigrating to Australia, another says that he moved to New York, where he changed his name and later married a wealthy woman. According to this telling, Dyson's wife died in mysterious circumstances in 1916, and he was suspected of murdering her, although he was never charged. Without further details, it is impossible to substantiate the story.

Susan Eubanks

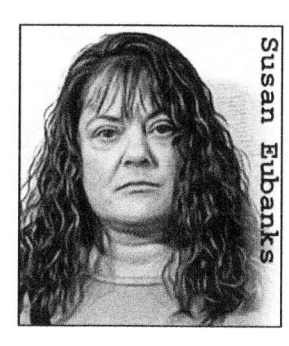

On the afternoon of Sunday, October 27, 1996, a man named Rene Dodson placed a 911 call from a gas station in San Marcos, California. According to Dodson, his girlfriend had taken his car keys and locked him out of their shared home. He wanted the police to respond to the scene and retrieve the keys for him so that he could leave. He then gave the address, a place that local officers were well acquainted with. They had responded to countless domestic violence incidents there.

The girlfriend that Dodson was referring to was a woman named Susan Eubanks, who lived at the property with her four sons, Brandon Armstrong, 14; Austin Eubanks, 7; Brigham Eubanks, 6; and Matthew Eubanks, age 4. The three younger boys had been fathered by Susan's second husband, Eric, but the couple had been living apart for nine months. They were currently headed for the divorce courts over allegations by Susan that her husband physically abused her. Some of those were proven, and Susan had been granted a restraining order. Eric had responded by accusing his wife of cheating on him.

None of that was relevant to the current situation, of course. Dodson was told to wait at the gas station for a police cruiser to arrive. A short while later, he was being driven to the house while explaining to the officers what had happened.

According to Dodson, he and Susan had been at the North Bar in Escondido that afternoon, watching a Chargers game on television. They'd been drinking heavily, and Susan had also been popping pills that had been prescribed for her due to a workplace injury. As was often the case when she was inebriated, Susan had become argumentative. The row had escalated during the afternoon and had continued even as the couple drove home. That was when Dodson had decided he'd had enough. He'd told Susan that they were through and that he was going to pack up his stuff and leave. In response, she'd started cussing him. As soon as he'd pulled the car into the drive, she'd reached over and grabbed his keys. Then she'd run into the house and locked the door. After several minutes trying to persuade her to let him in, Dodson had walked to the gas station and called 911.

The police cruiser was now pulling to a stop outside the Eubanks residence, and the officers could immediately see that Susan had not been idle during the intervening period. Two of the tires on Dodson's vehicle had been slashed. The headlights had also been turned on, possibly in an effort to run the battery down. Nonetheless, Susan was cooperative with the police officers, opening the door and allowing Dodson in to pack a suitcase. Since his car was incapacitated, the police agreed to give him a ride, but that turned out to be unnecessary. As they were leaving, Eric Eubank pulled up, summoned by a series of abusive calls from his ex-wife. He and Dodson left together, with the officers warning both of them not to return to the house.

The two men had no intention of disobeying that instruction. In fact, they headed straight for the North Bar, where Dodson and Susan had been drinking earlier that afternoon. There, over a few beers, they exchanged war stories. One, in particular, appeared ominous. According to Dodson, Susan had recently been threatening to commit suicide, saying that she was going to "take her boys with her" in order to get her revenge on her former husbands and all of the boyfriends who'd used and abused her. Eric was alarmed by this but not overly concerned. Whatever her other faults, Susan had always been a good mother. She doted on those boys.

But Eubanks would have cause to reevaluate that assessment just a few hours later. He was still at the bar when he received a voice message from Susan, an ominous message consisting of just two words, "Say goodbye." He immediately dialed 911 and asked for a patrol car to be sent to his wife's residence.

Deputies arrived at Susan Eubanks' ramshackle, two-bedroomed house at around 7:30 p.m. that evening. Their earlier visit had been routine. This one would be far different. They were just approaching the front door when they heard an anguished cry from within, a woman's voice calling out for help. Entering the residence, the officers almost immediately spotted 14-year-old Brandon Armstrong lying face down on the living room floor, a half-eaten bowl of cereal spilled around him. From the blood matted in his hair, it appeared that he'd been shot, and a cursory examination proved that this was the case. There were two bullet wounds to the head, either of which would have been fatal.

There was nothing that could be done for Brandon, and so the officers edged along the passage to the bedroom shared by the three younger boys. There, a bloodbath awaited them. Seven-year-old Austin was sitting upright on the top level of his bunk bed, dead from two bullets to the head. Brigham and Matthew, the younger boys, were on the bottom bunk, also with gunshot wounds to the head. A fifth child, the boys' five-year-old cousin, was also in the room, cowering in the corner, clearly traumatized but otherwise unharmed.

Austin and Brigham Eubanks, like their older half-brother Brandon, were clearly beyond help. But, miraculously, 4-year-old Matthew was still breathing. The officers therefore called in a medivac before proceeding to the main bedroom, following the anguished groans that had drawn them into the house in the first place. It was in that room that they found Susan Eubanks, crying in pain and clutching a blood-soaked towel to her midriff. She was rushed by ambulance to Palomar Medical Center where she received treatment for a bullet wound to the stomach. Meanwhile, Matthew was taken by helicopter to Children's Hospital in San Diego, where he was immediately placed on life support systems. Despite the best efforts of medical staff, he died at 4:30 p.m. on Monday, October 27. By then, the police had already found evidence in the house that pointed the finger directly at the killer. Five days after the shootings, Susan Eubanks was charged with four counts of first-degree murder.

The trial of Susan Eubanks eventually came before the courts in August of 1999. There, the prosecutor contended that the murders had been both callous and premeditated, an act of vengeance perpetrated by a woman who had wanted to get back at the men in her life. According to this theory, Rene Dodson's decision to end his relationship with the defendant had thrown her into a rage. She'd then taken her .38 revolver and carried out her shooting rampage, first executing Brandon as he sat watching television, then gunning down the younger boys as they played video games in their bedroom. It had not, however, been a spur of the moment thing. Eubanks had often spoken of shooting the boys to get back at those who had wronged her. As for the self-inflicted gunshot wound, the prosecution scoffed at the suggestion that this was a genuine suicide attempt. A woman who had cold-bloodedly gunned down four innocent children must surely have known how to kill herself. That, according to the prosecutor, had never been her intention. Rather, she'd been looking for a way to claim mitigation, or perhaps to blame the shootings on someone else.

The defense, quite understandably, offered a different version of events, the gist of it being that Susan had not been in full control of her faculties. She'd been under the influence of alcohol and prescription drugs and was not thinking clearly. Her reasoning abilities had also been impaired by multiple traumas – the loss of her nursing job due to her injury; the spousal abuse she'd suffered; abandonment by several boyfriends, most recently Rene Dodson; her precarious financial position which included over $40,000 in credit card debt. All of these factors had come together to form a perfect storm, which was then made worse by the consumption of drugs and alcohol. Given these conditions, it had only needed a spark to light the fuse. That spark had come with Rene Dodson's announcement that he was leaving. After that, Susan Eubanks had blacked out. She had been functioning with no more sentience than a "robot," according to her lawyer.

Unfortunately for the defense, its strategy was undermined by two pieces of evidence presented at the trial. The first was that Eubanks had reloaded her revolver twice during the shooting spree. That did not suggest someone who was operating on auto-pilot and unaware of what was going on. The second was no fewer than five "suicide notes" left by Eubanks. These were bile-filled letters addressed to the men who she felt had wronged her. Particularly telling was the note she'd left for her second husband, Eric. "You betrayed me," she'd written.

"I've lost everybody I've loved. Now, it's time for you to do the same."

The discovery of these notes was a death knell to the defense argument of diminished responsibility, since it was clear evidence of intent. At the start of the trial, the prosecutor had made an impassioned plea for the death penalty, stating that, "It was callous. It was cold. It was Susan Eubanks not being able to control the men anymore. So they had to suffer, even if it meant taking away the lives of four innocent children." Now the jury would have to decide whether Eubanks was guilty and whether she deserved to die for what she had done.

In the end, it took the jurors less than two hours to return a guilty verdict and only two days to recommend that Susan Eubanks should be put to death. Eubanks took the decision without emotion and left the courtroom in chains on October 13, 1999. She currently awaits execution at the Central California's Women's Facility in Chowchilla.

Clara Harris

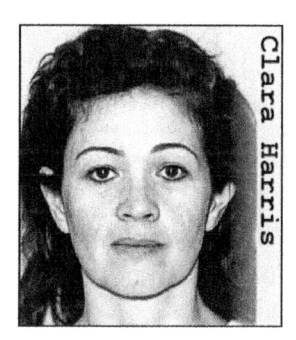

When Clara Harris called the Blue Moon Detective Agency on July 23, 2002, the story she had to tell was a familiar one. Tales of matrimonial strife are a familiar theme to private investigators, and catching cheating spouses is bread-and-butter work. In Clara's case, there was no real investigation to be done. Her husband, David, had admitted to her a week earlier that he had been sleeping with his former secretary, Gail Bridges. All she needed was for an investigator to tail David and to call her when he checked into a hotel for a tryst with his mistress. She would not have to wait long for that call.

David and Clara Harris were a golden couple. The pair were both qualified as dentists and operated a successful chain of orthodontic offices across Harris County, Texas. This allowed them to afford a comfortable lifestyle that included a luxury home in Friendswood, Texas, a couple of luxury cars in the garage, and regular vacations at exotic locations. On the family front, they also appeared to be happy. The couple had tied the knot on Valentine's Day 1993, and Clara had become stepmother to David's daughter, Lindsay. Three years later, they had children of their own, twin boys, born in 1996. To all the world, their life appeared to be just about perfect.

But all was not what it seemed. A decade into the marriage and David seemed to have lost interest in his wife sexually. Clara was by now approaching her mid-40s and, like many women in her age group, had begun to worry about losing her allure. David's constant rebuffs hurt her deeply, but she was still desperately in love with him and desperate to win back his affection. To this extent, she hired a personal trainer to get back her buff body, started shopping for sexy lingerie, even went to see a plastic surgeon about a breast enhancement. None of it worked. David appeared totally disinterested, and over time she began to suspect that he was having an affair. Then, after she'd eventually plucked up the courage to confront him, David had confirmed her worst fears. Yes, he was seeing someone, and to make matters worse, it was a former employee. Gail Bridges had once worked as a receptionist at one of their dental clinics.

Enter the Blue Moon Detective Agency. Clara was explicit in her instructions to them. They were to tail her husband and report back – not at the end of the assignment but in real time, as things were happening. Clara's plan was to confront David in public, causing him and the bimbo maximum embarrassment.

Thus it was that on the afternoon of Wednesday, July 24, 2002, Clara answered the phone and found a private investigator on the other end of the line. He was reporting in as instructed, letting her know that he had tailed her husband to the Nassau Bay Hilton in Houston, Texas, where he'd just entered in the company of a young woman. The detective also confirmed that David and the woman had taken a room at the hotel.

Clara had, of course, been expecting this news, but that didn't make it any easier to take. She'd had a week to absorb the fact that David was cheating and yet, somewhere in her brain, she'd harbored the vain hope that it was all somehow a mistake. Now there was no pretense that she could cling to. She was the cheated wife; deceived by the man she still loved; abandoned for a younger woman; made to feel unattractive and unwanted. A feeling of numbness enveloped her, dissipating quickly to be replaced by cold rage. Up until this moment, she'd wondered if she'd be able to go through with the public confrontation she had planned. Now there was no doubt. She was going to drive to the hotel; she was going to confront the adulterer; she was going to show him that she was not the kind of woman to be discarded on a whim.

Snatching up the keys of her Mercedes Benz, Clara Harris headed for the door. Then a thought occurred to her, a way to humiliate David even further. Standing in the doorway, she called up to David's daughter, Lindsay, asking if she'd like to go for a drive.

About twenty minutes later, Clara pulled her car into the parking lot of the Hilton. Instructing Lindsay to stay in the car, she headed for the hotel foyer where she demanded that staff call her husband and his mistress to the lobby. Her plan was still to confront David in public, causing him maximum embarrassment. But the minute she saw him and Gail exit the elevator, she lost control of her emotions. She waded in on Gail with hands flailing, claws out, grabbing a fistful of hair and another of blouse. A hotel security guard, standing close at hand, quickly intervened and separated the warring women. By then, Gail's blouse lay in tatters on the floor. The guard then restrained the squirming, cussing Clara. After confirming that neither David nor Gail wanted to involve the police, he marched Clara from the building and escorted her back to her car. He told her to leave and not to return unless she wanted to face trespassing charges.

Clara got back into her vehicle, her mood darker than ever. She ignored the questions that Lindsay directed at her and twisted the key in the ignition, gunning the engine in frustration. She was still sitting there moments later, when she saw David and Gail walk out of the hotel. As they headed across the parking lot towards David's Lincoln Navigator, a snap decision was made, one that would change all of their lives forever.

According to those who witnessed the incident, the Mercedes came racing across the parking lot "out of nowhere." David Harris must have heard the roar of its high-powered engine because he turned at the last moment, veering away from Gail. The car missed her but plowed into him, lifting him bodily from the ground before he crashed back down to the asphalt with a sickening crunch.

To the onlookers, the moment seemed to have occurred in slow motion. Now it was in freeze-frame – the high-revving sedan; the wild-eyed woman at the wheel; the man lying prone and injured on the ground. Then, to the horror of bystanders, the driver of the Mercedes made a tight turn and looped back, driving deliberately over the man's body as it lay on the ground. Then she did it again, crunching the man's bones under her wheels. Finally, she stopped the car with the body trapped underneath it. At that moment, the passenger door flew open and a teenage girl jumped from the vehicle. "My dad!" the girl screamed. "You've killed my dad!"

By the time police and emergency services arrived on the scene, David Harris was already dead from the multiple injuries he'd suffered. His wife Clara was still there, having made no effort to flee. It would have been pointless to do so anyway. Several witnesses had seen what had happened, including David's daughter Lindsay who'd been in the passenger seat of the death car. Even if that were not the case, the entire incident had been caught on video, ironically by the private eye who Clara had hired to catch her cheating husband.

Clara Harris was charged with murder and appeared in court in early 2003. In her initial statement to police and in press interviews, Clara had said that it had never been her intention to hit David. Her goal had been to "separate" him from Gail. That, of course, was a lie and there were several eyewitnesses to prove it. A new defense was called for, and Clara's attorney had one to offer the court. He insisted that his client had acted with "sudden passion," a momentary explosion of rage brought on by having her husband's infidelity confirmed. If accepted by the jury, this would act as mitigation of whatever sentence they chose to recommend, ranging from murder to negligent homicide. In the best case scenario, Clara Harris would serve no jail time at all.

As it turned out, the jury was prepared to accept the sudden passion defense. However, they chose to attach it to a murder conviction rather than a lesser charge. That meant that Clara Harris could receive a maximum of 20 years, and the jury recommended the maximum.

Despite the pleas of David Harris's parents, who testified on behalf of their daughter-in-law, Clara Harris was sentenced to 20 years behind bars. That sanction was handed down on February 14, 2003, the day that would have been her 11th anniversary.

FOOTNOTE: Clara Harris was released from prison on May 11, 2018.

Laurie Dann

In the aftermath of the tragedy, many would ask the question, why? Why did no one try to help this obviously disturbed woman? Why was she not red-flagged? Why was she not institutionalized? Why was such a deranged individual allowed to legally purchase not one, but three, firearms? Why?

The answers, if there are any, are elusive. Some relate to individual freedoms, others to misguided parental love, still others to societal indifference. The fact is that Laurie Wasserman Dann should have been in an institution long before that fateful day in May 1988, when she roamed the streets of Winnetka, Illinois, with her poisoned snacks, gasoline canister, and .32 Smith and Wesson revolver.

Laurie Wasserman was born on October 18, 1957, in Chicago, Illinois. Her father, Norman, was a successful accountant, and Laurie grew up in the affluent Chicago suburb of Glencoe. She wanted for nothing during her formative years, but she was an awkward, unattractive girl. That is, until her parents gave her the gift of plastic surgery. Under the point of the surgeon's knife, the ugly duckling was transformed into a beautiful, dark-haired girl, who was soon attracting suitors.

After graduating from New Trier East High School, Laurie was accepted at the University of Arizona and spent four years at study there, although she never graduated. That had never been the intention anyway. Laurie was attending college with the sole purpose of snaring a wealthy husband. She thought that she'd succeeded when she became engaged to a premed student. She was devastated when he ended the relationship. With very little interest in continuing her education in Arizona, she returned to her parents' home in 1980.

Still hurting from her failed relationship, Laurie had no particular plans for her future. She attended various adult education classes, but rarely finished a course. She also worked at a number of low-paying jobs, one of those as a waitress at the Green Acres Country Club in Northbrook. It was there that she met Russell Dann, a handsome young man from a wealthy Highland Park family.

Dann was immediately entranced by the pretty, dark-haired woman, and she was by no means averse to his attentions. The couple began dating, and married in September 1982, moving into a luxurious $230,000 Highland Park home.

However, wedded bliss was short-lived. Just days into the marriage, Russell began to realize that his new wife was no homemaker. He'd return from work to find the house a mess of unmade beds and dirty dishes piled up in the sink, while Laurie lay sprawled on the sofa watching TV. And on the occasions that she did make an attempt at housework, the results were unpredictable. One time she did the laundry, folded up the still wet clothing and packed it away in various closets. She also liked to keep things in odd places. Her makeup was stored in the microwave, for example, and she didn't use a purse to hold her cash. She simply scattered the notes and coins on the back seat of her car. And then there were her little rituals, like obsessive hand washing, and tapping her foot against the floor of her car every time she stopped at a traffic light.

Eventually, those behaviors would take their toll on the marriage, and the couple separated in October 1985. Divorce proceedings were acrimonious, with Laurie accusing Russell of spousal abuse. During this time, Russell and his family began to be harassed by hang-up phone calls.

In April 1986, Laurie accused her husband of breaking in and vandalizing her parents' home. Shortly after, she obtained a gun license and purchased a .357 Magnum. Then, in September 1986, Russell Dann was attacked in his house and stabbed with an ice pick while he slept. He pointed the finger at Laurie, but she denied the accusation and agreed to a polygraph, which she passed with flying colors. No charges were brought. Evidence would later emerge that Laurie had purchased an ice pick, similar to the one used to stab Russell, just days before the attack.

In May 1987, the Danns' marriage was officially dissolved, with Laurie banking a $125,000 settlement. But if Russell Dann thought that he'd seen the last of his ex-wife, he was sorely mistaken. She continued to make harassing calls to him and his family and to lay wild charges against him with the police. She claimed that he'd raped her with a steak knife and that he'd planted a bomb in her parents' home. No charges were officially laid against Russell, but Laurie's parents firmly believed her claims and continued to support her.

And Russell Dann wasn't the only target of Laurie's harassment. Her former boyfriend in Arizona reported to the police that she'd been making death threats against his family and claiming to be pregnant with his child, even though he'd last seen her over five years ago. She'd also sent an anonymous letter to the hospital where he worked, claiming to be a patient who had been raped by him. The harassment would continue until Norman Wasserman received a lawyer's letter, asking him to rein in his daughter.

In January 1987, Laurie posted a notice at the Glencoe public library and at a local grocery store offering her services as a babysitter. One mother, obviously unaware of her history, offered her a job and found her to be pleasant, soft-spoken, and excellent with children. She was soon recommending Laurie to her friends.

But, as with everything in Laurie Dann's life, the veneer of sanity soon wore thin. Parents began to notice disarranged objects in their homes after Laurie had been there, slashes to rugs and sofas, small objects missing. One couple went as far as filing a police complaint, but there was no hard evidence and no charges were brought. Nonetheless, Laurie's once thriving babysitting business soon ground to a halt.

In the summer of 1987, Laurie delighted her parents by announcing that she was returning to college to complete her degree. Norman Wasserman, as ever attentive to his daughter's needs, rented her a university apartment in Evanston, Illinois. It wasn't long before students were complaining about raw meat being left to rot under cushions in common rooms, and about garbage pushed into their mailboxes. The culprit was soon identified. Norman Wasserman was politely asked to remove his daughter from the university.

And he was soon dealing with a new crisis of his daughter's making. Duping a new set of mothers into hiring her as a babysitter, she began causing damage to their property and stealing hundreds of dollars worth of food. Norman, as always, covered her tracks, paying restitution and pleading with her victims not to file charges. Nobody did.

It seems strange that Norman Wasserman, so attentive to his daughter's needs, did not comprehend what in retrospect seems obvious. Laurie Dann needed psychiatric care. She needed to be institutionalized. Instead, she was allowed to strike out on her own again in January of 1988. This time, she moved to Madison and enrolled at the University of Wisconsin.

All too soon, Laurie's strange behavior began to attract attention. In addition to her old habit of leaving raw meat to rot wherever she went, she developed a compulsion for riding the elevator at all times of the day and night. She also took to wearing rubber gloves and shying away from metal surfaces. She was seen on occasion wandering the halls naked, but most of the time she barricaded herself in her dorm room, which she turned into a health hazard, with rotting food and garbage everywhere.

In the fall of 1987, Dann again reported her ex-husband to the police. She claimed that he'd written threatening letters and that he'd sexually assaulted her in a parking lot. When her story wasn't believed, she became angry. A few weeks later, she purchased a second revolver, a .32-caliber Smith and Wesson.

In March 1988, Dann started making preparations for the attacks she'd eventually carry out. She began stealing library books on poisons and pilfering arsenic from the chemistry lab. She also started a concerted shoplifting operation, accumulating clothes and wigs that she intended using to disguise herself. During this time, she also escalated her campaign of threatening phone calls, targeting the Dann family, her ex-boyfriend, and her former babysitting clients. Also in March, she was arrested for shoplifting but avoided jail time.

She was suspected of arson in April, after a fire started in one of the dorm rooms at the university. No charges were brought. In the meantime, an FBI investigation had been launched into the death threats made against her Arizona boyfriend. During the course of that inquiry, it was determined that Dann legally owned three firearms. When the police arrived at the Wasserman residence to request the voluntary surrender of the weapons, Norman Wasserman refused. He insisted that his daughter needed the guns for protection against her ex-husband.

By now, Laurie Dann's descent into madness had passed the tipping point. On May 14, a student at the university returned to find that his clothing and books had been shredded. Laurie was implicated and a search was launched for her. She was found later that night, sleeping naked in a pile of garbage, covered only by a plastic bag. Before any disciplinary action could be launched, she disappeared from the campus and returned to Glencoe. The end game was in play. Laurie Dann was preparing for a massacre.

On the evening of May 19, 1988, Dann stayed up late, making rice crispy snacks laced with arsenic and injecting poison into pre-packaged fruit juice. The following morning, she mailed several packages of the poisoned snacks to former acquaintances, babysitting clients, and to her psychiatrist. She then personally delivered her toxic treats to a number of homes in Glencoe as well as to various fraternity houses at Northwestern University in Evanston.

Then, she went to pick up the sons of one of her babysitting clients for a prearranged day out. Leaving the residence, she drove to Ravinia Elementary School, where her former sister-in-law's children were pupils. There she started a fire, before fleeing. Next, she drove to the daycare center that her ex-sister-in-law's daughter attended. Her plan was to start another fire, but a staff member saw her carrying a gasoline can and told her to leave.

A short while later, Dann returned the boys to their home. She gave them each a glass of milk, but they refused to drink it, saying it tasted funny (the milk was later positively tested for arsenic). She then brought the boys down to the basement where their mother was doing laundry. She mumbled some excuse as to why she'd had to cancel the day out and then left. Moments later, the children's mother smelled smoke. She went to investigate and saw that the basement stairs were ablaze. She and her sons escaped by breaking a small window and crawling to safety.

Dann had meanwhile entered the nearby Hubbard Woods Elementary School, carrying a gun in each hand, like a movie assassin. Seeing a boy exiting a washroom, she shot at him, hitting him in the stomach. Next, she entered a second-grade classroom and began firing wildly. Eight-year-old Nicholas Corwin was killed instantly. Five others were critically injured.

Thankfully, Dann did not venture any further into the school. She fled in her car, traveling just a few blocks before colliding with a tree. Then she reloaded her weapons, left the vehicle, and entered the home of the Andrews family. She claimed that she had shot a man who had raped her and that the police were now hunting her. She needed a place to hide out.

Over the next six hours, Dann held the family hostage. During that time, she made a call to her mother, who begged her to turn herself in. Laurie said she'd think about it.

Eventually, Phillip Andrews, 20, convinced her to let the rest of his family go, while he remained as a hostage. Laurie agreed, but as soon as the family was safe, Phillip tried to wrestle the gun away. A shot was fired, hitting him in the chest. He staggered out of the house and collapsed on the front lawn.

With the police closing in on the house, Laurie Dann then climbed the stairs to an upstairs bedroom, put her revolver in her mouth, and blew her own brains out.

Laurie Dann's rampage had left an eight-year-old boy dead, and seven people seriously injured. Several others had to be treated for arsenic poisoning, smoke inhalation, and other injuries. Still others had to receive trauma counseling.

In the wake of the tragedy, it was revealed that Dann had been seeing psychiatrists for obsessive-compulsive disorders for many years. She was also thought to be suffering from "erotomania," a tendency towards forming pathological attachments to men she believed were in love with her. She'd been taking both lithium and anafranil. Both drugs can cause violence in patients.

Gay Oakes

The first time that Gay Oakes laid eyes on Doug Gardner, he was laying waste to a bar in Sydney, Australia, acting out in a drunken rage. That should have acted as a warning to the unwed mother of two, but instead she found herself attracted to the rugged New Zealander. Soon the two of them had shacked up together, along with Gay's two children. It was then that she started to appreciate the true nature of the man she'd fallen in love with. Doug Gardner was a violent drunk, a habitual gambler, a pathological liar. He was also insanely jealous and would accuse Gay of infidelity on the flimsiest of evidence or on no evidence at all. Denials only made things worse and led to savage beatings with fists and feet. The local constabulary became well acquainted with the Gardner/Oakes homestead. They were called there frequently.

And yet, despite this maltreatment, Gay Oakes made no move to leave her abusive partner. In fact, over the first four years of their relationship, she allowed him to impregnate her twice, inextricably tying their life histories together. Still, there were chances to escape, most notably in 1987 when Gardner abandoned her and the children and returned to his native New Zealand. Left destitute and with four young mouths to feed, Oakes was nonetheless distraught at the loss of her abusive lover. She prayed that he would return to her, and those prayers, perverse though they were, were answered when she received a letter from Doug. He told her that he still loved her and begged her to bring the children and join him in Christchurch. Oakes almost tripped over herself on the way to pack her bags.

Gardner's letter had struck a conciliatory note. He'd told Gay that he'd given up drinking and had decided to get his life together. He realized that he'd treated her badly and he was determined to mend his ways. Could she ever forgive him? Gay, of course, could forgive, but she should have known better. The reunion may have been tearful and the first few weeks blissful, but all too soon the old Doug was back. The lazy, unreliable, dishonest Doug, the Doug who beat her and stole from her, the Doug who was frequently drunk and who gambled away her housekeeping money. He even (according to a book later published by Oakes) started sexually abusing her oldest daughter.

So what did Gay Oakes do? Did she walk out on this intolerably cruel man? Did she pack up her children and return to Australia? Did she finally accept that Doug Gardner was rotten to the core, beyond redemption, a lost cause? No, she did none of those things. In fact, she stayed with Gardner, even bearing him two more children over the next six years. When she finally did end the relationship, it was not by walking out on him. It was by stirring 60 ground-up sleeping pills into his coffee.

In January 1993, Oakes called a friend named Jo and told her that she urgently needed her help. Jo asked no questions before rushing over to the Gardner/Oakes residence. There she found an unresponsive Doug Gardner lying on the bedroom floor. According to Gay, she had put sleeping pills into his coffee in an effort to knock him out. Her intention had not been to kill, she said, but rather to gain some respite from his constant abuse. After Doug had passed out, she'd dragged him into the bedroom to let him sleep it off. When she checked on him the next morning, he was still asleep. However, after going out to do some shopping, she'd returned to find that he was no longer breathing. That was when she'd called Jo.

The two women were now left with a problem. Gay quickly overruled Jo when the latter suggested calling the police. "They'll lock me up," she said. "They'll take my kids away." Which left only one option. They were going to have to get rid of the body. That was achieved by dragging Doug out into the garden, digging a large hole and burying him in it.

There were questions raised about Gardner's sudden disappearance, of course, not least by his family. Unable to get a satisfactory answer out of Gay, they eventually went to the police and reported Doug missing. Questioned regarding her partner's whereabouts, Gay said that he had abandoned her, just as he'd done in Australia six years earlier. The police were willing to accept that story. It would be fourteen months before they considered an alternative solution to their missing person case. That was when an anonymous caller suggested that they do some digging in Gay Oates's backyard. Those excavations would turn up the decomposed remains of the missing man.

Gay Oates was arrested and charged with murder. At her September 1994 trial, her attorney offered two mitigating arguments. The first was that Gay had not intended murder. Her crime was in miscalculating the dosage she had given her victim. But that theory was destroyed by the autopsy report which suggested that Gardner had consumed between 60 and 70 sleeping pills. That quantity of pills could not have been mixed into a single cup of coffee. Oates must have been doping him with medication over at least a couple of days.

The second justification offered by Oates was controversial, especially for the era. She claimed that spousal abuse, over an extended period of time, had led her to murder. Modern studies suggest that victims who are exposed to sustained abuse lose the ability to think rationally and may therefore be incapable of determining right from wrong. But if this was the case with Gay Oates, why had she gone to such great lengths to conceal the body? Why had she lied to the police? Clearly, these were the actions of someone who understood that what she had done was wrong and had taken extraordinary steps to conceal her unlawful act.

That, in any case, was how the jury called it. In September 1994, Gay Oates was found guilty of murder and sentenced to life in prison. Under New Zealand law, she would have to spend at least ten years behind bars before she'd be eligible for parole. An appeal was then launched, again citing "battered woman syndrome" as a mitigating circumstance. To the ire of women's groups throughout the country, it was rejected. Oates would remain incarcerated for the minimum term at least.

Gay Oates turned out to be a model prisoner. And her stay behind bars would be less than the ten-year minimum. Attitudes towards spousal abuse were changing, and in 2002, the parole board agreed to hear a petition from Oates's representatives. That hearing resulted in the convicted murderess being released. She had served just eight years behind bars.

Inez Palmer

Inez Palmer was just 21 years old when she was hired to work as a live-in helper to the ailing Mrs. Sarah Stout of Vinton County, Ohio, in 1923. She was a pretty, spirited girl, and it did not take long before she attracted the attention of Mrs. Stout's widowed 30-year-old son Arthur. The two quickly became lovers and Inez quit her post and moved with Arthur into a shack he occupied on his father's considerable acreage. Over the next three years, she and Arthur lived as man and wife, cohabiting "without the benefit of the clergy," in the parlance of the day.

This arrangement was a source of great distress to Sarah. A deeply religious woman, she was vocal in her criticism of her stepson's conduct, and this caused ongoing tension between them. She frequently asked her husband, William, to intercede and talk sense into his son. William's failure to do so only served to heighten the tensions in the family. On November 17, 1926, those tensions eventually came to a head. That was the day that a young neighbor, Manville Perry, was passing the Stout farmhouse and noticed the living room door standing ajar. Peering in, he observed a scene he'd never forget. He immediately ran to a nearby coal mine to ask for help.

Perry soon returned to the house in the company of several burly and soot-blackened miners. Entering the property, the men found Sarah Stout's charred corpse lying in front of the living room stove. Her face, neck and upper body had been burnt beyond recognition. Even in their state of shock, the miners could see that something was not right with the picture. It appeared that Mrs. Stout had made no attempt to extinguish the flames, even as they'd engulfed her. One of the men went immediately to call the sheriff.

Sheriff Maude Collins was an anomaly in the male-dominated 1920s, the first female sheriff in Vinton County's history and quite possibly the first in the nation. "Sheriff Maude" had assumed the post after her husband, Sheriff Fletcher Collins, was shot and killed during a routine traffic stop. But she was no mere figurehead, appointed to complete her husband's term. In fact, she proved so adept at the job that she was re-elected in her own right once her proxy term was done. She would achieve national fame for the work she did on the Stout case.

The initial impression formed by the sheriff was that the victim had been placed in front of the stove and lit on fire while either unconscious or already dead. This theory would be supported by Dr. O. S. Cox and Dr. A. E. James, who conducted the autopsy. Their conclusion was that the 60-year-old woman had been strangled, her body then posed in front of the stove, doused with kerosene and torched.

But who would have done such a dreadful thing? Suspicion fell almost immediately on Arthur Stout, whose clashes with his stepmother were no secret. In fact, it was learned that Sarah Stout had driven into McArthur, two days before her death, and had laid formal adultery charges against her stepson, citing his illicit relationship with Inez Palmer. That had led to his arrest, but he had soon walked free after his father paid his bail.

So Arthur had been free at the time of his stepmother's murder and he had motive. But had he actually committed the crime? One clue might have been an unhitched wagon standing in the yard of the Stout residence. A team of bloodhounds was brought in, and they immediately picked up Arthur Stout's scent from the wagon and followed it into the house, to the exact spot where his stepmother had been found. With his father demanding that he be arrested and punished, Arthur was taken into custody and charged with murder. Later, the old man would have a change of heart, hiring a local lawyer to represent his son. The efforts of that attorney could not prevent a Grand Jury indicting Arthur for first degree murder.

With Arthur behind bars and Sarah dead, the other two players in the drama turned to each other for solace. William Stout Sr. had taken in Arthur's two young sons, Artie and William, and needed someone to care for them; Inez was in need of some form of financial support. The solution was simple. Inez moved into the Stout farmhouse as a caregiver to the boys and a housekeeper to William. As a domestic arrangement, it would be of very short duration. In February 1927, William Stout Sr. disappeared.

William Stout was a well-to-do and well-respected farmer, and so it did not take long before his disappearance was noted. When the sheriff arrived at his Axtel Ridge farmstead, asking questions about his whereabouts, Inez Palmer said that she'd last seen him mending fences on the property. She also mentioned that he'd been acting strangely since his wife's death and had been speaking of "heading out west."

That sounded odd to Sheriff Collins, but she asked no further questions of Palmer. Instead, she and her deputy, Ray Cox, did a circuit of the

Stout property, following the fence and hoping to find the location where William had last been working. About two-and-a-half miles from the farmhouse, they found a lunch pail under a tree. The pail contained a handwritten will. In it, William Stout named Arthur as his sole heir, disinheriting his other two sons. The will was signed (apparently by William) but it had not been witnessed.

Also at the site, the police officers noticed a curious set of footprints, leading to and from the lunch pail. Sheriff Maude examined the footprints, then decided to compare the size and imprint to those of the missing man. A pair of William Stout's shoes were then retrieved from the farmhouse and found to fit the prints exactly. What was odd, though, was that the prints were quite shallow. Deputy Cox, a man of about the same stature as Stout, made much deeper impressions in the soil. Acting on a hunch, Sheriff Maude then put on the shoes herself. The prints she made matched those left at the scene. The implication was obvious. Whoever had left those prints weighed considerably less than William Stout.

With a theory already half-formed in her mind, Sheriff Maude headed back to the farmhouse. A quick search of the premises revealed that Stout had taken none of his belongings. If he really had "headed west," as Inez had suggested, he'd done so with no more than the clothes on his back. The sheriff next drove into McArthur and presented the will to the cashier at Vinton County National Bank, where William Stout had his account. A comparison of the handwriting proved what Maude already suspected. The will was a forgery.

Inez Palmer seemed surprised when Sheriff Maude and her deputy returned to the farmhouse the next day. But the sheriff soon put her at ease, telling her that they were just there to look for clues as to where William might have gone. In truth, Maude wanted to question William Stout's young grandsons, Artie and William. Perhaps they'd seen or heard something? As it turned out they hadn't. They had, however, been given a stern warning by Inez Palmer. She'd told them not to drink from the well at the rear of the property. She'd told them that the water was tainted.

And that turned out to be a valid warning. The water was indeed contaminated. The well contained the dead body of William Stout Sr. The elderly Stout had been bludgeoned to death, the blows delivered with such force that they had fractured his skull in several places.

Inez Palmer was arrested and charged with murder. Once in custody, she quickly confessed, claiming that she had killed William in self-defense after he had made advances toward her. She'd then attempted to cover up the crime by putting on a pair of her victim's shoes and making the footprints near the repaired fences to back up her story. She also admitted that she'd forged the will, offering the ludicrous explanation that since William Stout was dead anyway, she didn't see why she and Arthur shouldn't benefit.

Sheriff Maude Collins had just solved her first murder and would become somewhat of a national hero once the story was featured in True Detective magazine. But the case still had a few twists to deliver. When Arthur Stout was told of his lover's confession, he decided to come clean about his involvement in his stepmother's murder. According to Arthur, it was Inez who had killed Sarah, not him. He'd only assisted in the disposal of the body.

Arthur would later change his version of events, saying that Sarah's murder had been his father's idea, after she'd brought shame on the family by laying charges of adultery. Whether that was true or not, it did not save him from the justice he deserved. Found guilty of second-degree murder, he was sentenced to life in prison. Inez was also found guilty, although in her case, the conviction was for first-degree murder. She, too, was sentenced to life behind bars.

Barbara Opel

Greg Heimann had not seen his father Jerry in five years. It wasn't that he had a problem with the old guy, just that time and distance had kept them apart. Greg lived in Arkansas, his father in Everett, Washington. It would take a crisis to eventually bring them together in April 2001. At 64, Jerry had recently been diagnosed with cancer and, true to form, was refusing treatment. Greg had come west to persuade him otherwise.

Greg had landed at Seattle's Sea-Tac Airport on the afternoon of April 15, 2001. He had arranged for his father to pick him up from the airport, but Jerry wasn't there when he arrived and did not show up over the next three-and-a-half hours. Perhaps he'd decided that he didn't want to listen to his son's advice after all. Not that the no-show was going to discourage Greg from his purpose. If his father wasn't going to come to him, then he'd have to go to his father. Hailing a cab, he headed for the address.

Greg arrived to find the house in darkness, the shades drawn and all of the doors locked. Knocking brought no response from within, and so he eventually decided to break in. It was through a small side window that he gained access. What he found inside only ratcheted up his level of concern. His 89-year-old grandmother was sitting unattended in her wheelchair, shredded pages from a magazine stuffed in her mouth. The old lady suffered from Alzheimer's, and Greg could get no sense from her as to what had happened. It was apparent, though, that something had happened. The house was entirely devoid of furniture. To his consternation, he also found spots of dried blood on a garbage can and on a chandelier. What had happened here? Greg didn't know, but he clung to the hope that there must be some rational explanation. After attending to his grandmother, he sat down to wait for his father's return. It did not come that night.

The following day, Greg decided to launch a search for his missing father. By now, his emotions were a mix of annoyance and apprehension. He could not believe that his father would have left his elderly grandmother unattended, yet couldn't help wondering if the old man had gone out on one of his drinking binges. Perhaps he was, even now, falling down drunk in some dive or shacked up with some bimbo. It wouldn't be the first time that had happened. Still, that didn't explain the missing furniture. And hadn't his dad recently hired a live-in caregiver to take care of his ailing grandmother? If so, where was she? With these thoughts swirling around in his mind, Greg set off to visit all of his father's regular haunts. Jerry wasn't at any of them. In fact, no one had seen him in a couple of days. It was then that Greg decided to go to the police.

The mystery of Jerry Heimann's disappearance would eventually be solved six days later when his body was found discarded beside a road on the Tulalip Indian reservation. The corpse was wrapped in bloodstained sheets, and acid had been poured over it in an apparent attempt to prevent identification. By not even the acid burns could hide the horrendous injuries the victim had suffered. Jerry had been bludgeoned and stabbed to death, and the evidence pointed to more than one assailant.

This was not a cleverly executed crime. From the very start the police only had one suspect. Barbara Opel was a pudgy, 39-year-old mother-of-three who had been hired by Heimann in the Fall of 2000 to care for his ailing mother. She was brash and uncouth, and neighbors often heard her and Jerry involved in shouting matches. Now Jerry was dead and Opel and her brood - aged 13, 11, and 7 - were missing, along with most of her employer's possessions. It did not take a genius to pull the strands together or to find the suspect. Opel had recently used Jerry Heimann's credit card to check into a motel, and that was where the police found her. She was soon in custody, and it was then that investigators learned the dreadful truth. Barbara Opel had not committed the murder herself. Instead, she had hired a gang of teenagers to do her dirty work. One of the killers was her 13-year-old daughter, Heather.

Heather, as it turned out, was more than just a killer. She had also been her mother's recruiter. The plot to kill Jerry Heimann had actually been hatched months earlier when Jerry had made $40,000 on the sale of a property and Barbara had decided that she wanted the money for herself. Over the following weeks, she'd made several indiscreet and ill-advised comments to complete strangers, suggesting that there might be some money in it if they could point her in the direction of a hitman. When these blundering efforts failed, Barbara struck on a new idea. Heather had been agitating for a dirt bike. "You can have the bike," Barbara told the 13-year-old. "But only if you kill Jerry."

Thus was the plot set in motion. In March of 2001, Heather recruited a 14-year-old friend, Marriam Oliver, and three adolescent boys. The teens then met with Barbara who offered them $300 each for carrying out the murder. She also told them how she wanted it done. They were to hide in the house armed with baseball bats and were to attack Jerry as he arrived home from one of his benders. He'd be falling down drunk, she assured them, and easy to subdue. That plan was, in fact, put in motion. But at the last moment, the teenagers lost their nerve and didn't spring the attack.

Barbara was annoyed that her juvenile killers had failed to follow through. Within days, however, she'd have a second hit squad assembled, this one more reliable than the first. At the center of this group was a muscular 17-year-old named Jeff Grote. Heather Opel had a crush on Grote and had recently plucked up the courage to slip him a suggestive note. Soon after, the two of them were involved in a sexual relationship, with Barbara even providing her 13-year-old daughter with a private bedroom where she and Grote could have sex. She also began pestering Grote to assemble a murder team for her, promising him a car in exchange. Soon Grote had recruited his friend Kyle Boston, 15, and Boston's 13-year-old cousin, Mike. Heather Opel and Marriam Oliver rounded out the group. Then Kyle, Mike and Marriam were each promised $300 for their part in the murder. Grote would get a car and Heather would get her dirt bike. The date was set for April 13.

Jerry Heimann was a man of regular habits. The Boeing retiree spent most evenings at one of his regular watering holes, usually arriving home in an inebriated state. April 13, 2001, was no different. Sitting in the darkened lounge with her juvenile team of assassins, Barbara Opel saw the sweep of Jerry's truck lights and instructed Heather to get her friends into position. Then she scuttled off to the basement with her younger children. Losing her nerve at the last moment, Marriam Oliver tried to follow, but Barbara sent her back upstairs with a rebuke. "Get back up there and do what you're supposed to do," she hissed into the darkness. "You're supposed to be Heather's friend. You're supposed to be there for her." The girl meekly complied. Moments later, Jerry Heimann entered the house and the first blow was struck.

Later, investigators would be able to reconstruct the horrific events from the confessions of the offenders. Heimann had just stepped into the residence when he was struck by an aluminum baseball bat swung by Jeff Grote. He collapsed immediately to the floor. "Who are you?" the 64-year-old cried out. "What do you want?" All he got in reply was another meaty blow. Then the other two boys joined the fray, swinging mini-bats branded with the name of the local MLB team, the Seattle Mariners. They continued this assault for several minutes, ignoring Heimann's piteous cries for mercy. Finally, the girls, Heather and Marriam, joined in, passing a 10-inch kitchen knife between them and taking turns to stab the stricken man. "That was fun!" Heather exclaimed as their victim lay dying. "I want to do that again."

Barbara Opel had been cowering in the basement during the attack, but now she emerged to take control of the situation. She immediately put the children, including her 7 and 11 year olds, to work mopping up blood and cleaning up the scene. Then she got the older boys to wrap the body in a sheet and load it into the victim's car. It would later be dumped beside a road on the outskirts of Everett. That done, Opel drove her teenaged killing crew to a fast food restaurant and treated them to a celebratory meal. She and her family stayed that night at a motel. The following day, she arrived at Jerry Heimann's house with a rental truck, paid for with his credit card. She then loaded up all of his possessions. Through all of this, Jerry's mother, the 89-year-old invalid that Opel had been hired to care for, was left unattended. She would remain in her wheelchair, confused and unfed, for two days before Greg Heimann broke in and rescued her.

By any definition, this was a cruel and shocking crime, made more so by the tender ages of the participants. It was also stunningly stupid. There was zero chance that Barbara Opel would have gotten away with it. She was soon charged with first-degree murder. From the very start, prosecutors made it clear that they would be seeking the death penalty for Opel and would seek to try the other perpetrators as adults.

Barbara Opel appeared in court in April 2003. Typical of the woman, she sought to shift the blame, naming her 13-year-old daughter as the prime mover in the murder plot. No one in the courtroom, least of all the jury, was buying that. They found Opel guilty of murder and sentenced her to life in prison without parole. She only escaped execution because some jurors balked at the idea of sending a woman to death row. "You're an evil piece of trash," Greg Heimann told Opel as he addressed her during the victim impact session. Few in the courtroom would have disagreed.

As for the other defendants, Jeff Grote got 50 years; Heather Opel and Marriam Oliver each got 22 years; and Kyle Boston got 18 years. Only 13-year-old Mike Boston was tried as a juvenile. He was remanded to a juvenile facility where he will remain until age 21.

Eva Dugan

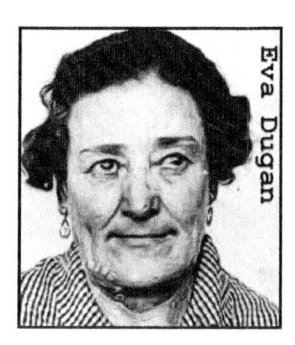

Born in 1876, Eva Dugan endured a childhood of want and degradation before finally hitting the road in her teens. She soon found herself joining the Klondike Gold Rush that was at the time attracting tens of thousands of prospectors to the frigid Yukon in northwestern Canada. Eva didn't find gold there, but she did find thousands of lonely men, desperate for some female attention. Many of the women in the camps worked as prostitutes, but Eva had another saleable asset. She had a fine singing voice and started performing as a cabaret singer, eventually taking her act to Juneau, Alaska. Only 16 at the time, she married and soon had two children to care for. Then, after her husband abandoned her and the kids, she was placed in a precarious position. She'd always sworn that she'd never sell herself on the streets. Now she was forced into it.

We lose track of Eva around the turn of the century and only pick up her trail again in late 1926 in Arizona. By now, she was in her early 50s, and whatever looks she'd once possessed were long gone. Not much else had changed, though. She was still living a shiftless life, still barely keeping body and soul together. In November of that year, she'd been hired to work as a housekeeper for a retired chicken rancher named Andrew Mathis. She'd had little competition for the job. Locals refused to work for Mathis, who was known to be demanding, cranky, and a cheapskate. Many of his employees quit in tears after just a few days, but Eva was made of sterner stuff. The two were frequently at each other's throats. If Mathis insulted Eva, she directed a barb right back at him. If he threatened violence, she dared him to try. Mathis even told a friend that he believed Eva was trying to poison him.

It was a situation that was never going to endure for very long, and in January of 1927, Mathis had finally had enough. After one row too many, he fired Eva and told her to leave his property immediately. An acquaintance of Mathis's, who was present during this exchange, would later testify that Eva did not appear too upset about her dismissal. She'd simply walked from the room without saying a word.

But a few days later, Eva was still living at the ranch. In fact, she was now telling the locals that she owned it. Her unlikely story was that Mathis had decided he wanted to live out the rest of his life in California and had departed immediately, leaving all of his possessions and property to his one-time maid. Neighbors, who knew that Mathis seldom parted with a penny if he could help it, found it hard to believe that he would have willingly turned over his ranch to a woman who had only worked for him for a couple of months. Then Eva started offering Mathis's livestock for sale, and his friends decided to go to the police and report him missing.

Eva, however, was one step ahead of them. When deputies arrived at the ranch the next morning, they found the place deserted and no sign of either the rancher or his housekeeper. A search was then conducted and turned up some worrying evidence. An ear trumpet used by the hard-of-hearing Mathis was found charred and discarded in a stove; Mathis's clothes were found strewn around the place; the cover of his Dodge roadster lay in the front yard, spattered with what looked like blood. Of the vehicle, itself, there was no trace.

A search was now launched for the fugitive housekeeper, but it produced no results until the authorities learned that Eva had a daughter living in White Plains, New York. Sure enough, a stakeout of the premises revealed that she was living there. Taken into custody, Eva denied knowing anything about her former employer's whereabouts. She had no defense against the charge of auto theft, though, and was therefore extradited back to Arizona. Convicted, she was sentenced to a three-to-six-year term at the state penitentiary. With good behavior, she'd probably have been out in 18 months.

But although Eva Dugan's behavior was exemplary behind bars, she would never earn parole. Nearly a year after Andrew Mathis went missing, a man was camping on the Mathis ranch when he noticed an unusual depression on the ground. Curious, the camper started scraping away at the dirt and soon unearthed skeletal remains. Andrew Mathis was identified by the clothes he was wearing. An autopsy would reveal that he'd died of a severe skull fracture, most probably inflicted with an axe.

Of course, there was only one suspect, and the police did not have to go far to find her. Confronted with the discovery, Eva scoffed at the allegations of murder. "If I'd killed him," she said. "I'd have buried him so deep that you'd never have found him." Pressed further, she finally admitted that she might know who had killed Mathis, although she insisted that she, herself, had nothing to do with the murder. "It was a feller named Jack," she said, before launching into a story that was her most fantastic yet.

According the Eva, Jack was a young man who she'd met at a local diner. The two of them struck up a conversation, and she was so touched by his hard luck story that she suggested he head out to the Mathis ranch and ask Andrew Mathis for a job. Jack did exactly that and was hired on the spot.

But he soon fell foul of his employer's notoriously short fuse. On his first day on the job, Jack was told to milk the cows but was unable to do so, having never worked on a farm before. This greatly annoyed Mathis who first berated the young man and then struck him in the face. Jack then fought back, landing a blow that caused Mathis to fall and strike his head. He never got up. Despite Jack and Eva's desperate efforts to revive him, it was soon apparent that he was dead. Eva then wanted to call the sheriff, but Jack stopped her from doing so. He insisted that she help him to load the body in the car. If she refused, he would simply hit the road, leaving her to face the music on her own.

According to Dugan, she had reluctantly helped dispose of the body. She'd then decided that it might be best to get out of town. Questions would undoubtedly be asked about Mathis's disappearance. Questions to which she had no answers. That was the only reason she'd taken her employer's car, she said.

The story was delivered with a seasoned liar's flair for embellishment. Unfortunately for Eva, it was also full of holes. The biggest of these was Jack. No one could be found who had seen the young man, and the police suspected from the start that he was no more than a fiction, created by Dugan to avoid responsibility for the murder. Or perhaps she was thinking ahead to her trial, perhaps she was trying lay the ground for an acquittal on reasonable doubt.

If that was her intention, it didn't work. Tried and found guilty, she was sentenced to death. Defiant to the end, she told the jurors in her final statement: "Well, at least I'll die with my boots on. That's more than most of you old coots will be able to boast on." She would maintain that upbeat stance during her time on death row, leading Time magazine to call her "Cheerful Eva" in an article it published about her execution on March 3, 1930. In the meanwhile, her lawyers had filled a clemency appeal on grounds of mental incompetence. Dugan was afflicted with advanced syphilis, and two doctors were put on the stand to testify that her mental state was impaired by the disease. That appeal was rejected, with the execution set for February 21, 1930.

Eva Dugan would be the first (and only) woman put to death by the state of Arizona. Her execution was also the first in which female witnesses were allowed into the death chamber as observers. Four women were seated among the 30 when Dugan climbed the stairs to the gallows at 5 a.m. on February 21. They were about to witness a spectacle every bit as bloody as the murder Eva Dugan had been convicted of.

Hanging a condemned person is both an art and a science. The length of the drop has to be calculated just right for the prisoner's weight. Done correctly, this will snap the neck at soon as the body hits the end of the rope, causing instant death. Calculate the drop too short, though, and the prisoner strangles to death. The consequences of a too-long drop are even more catastrophic. That is exactly what happened in the case of Eva Dugan.

Dugan approached her death stoically, even instructing the guards not to hold her arms too tightly, lest the onlookers conclude that she was afraid to die. She climbed to her place of dying with an unfaltering step, although she did sway slightly as the noose was placed around her neck. Asked whether she had any final words, she simply shook her head. At 5:11 a.m., the trap was sprung.

But the drop was too long and, as usually happens in such cases, the head was ripped from the body. It rolled across the floor, spewing blood from severed arteries before coming to rest just a few feet from the spectators. Several of those scrambled away from the grisly scene while five witnesses – two of them women – fell into a faint.

In the aftermath of the botched execution, there was a public outcry leading to the gallows being replaced by the gas chamber as the preferred method of execution in Arizona. It left Eva Dugan with two dubious distinctions. She was the last person hanged in the state and the only woman it ever judicially executed.

The case of Eva Dugan would continue to hold the public interest for years to come, with several outrageous stories doing the rounds.

Among these were two that bear repeating. One was that Eva had been married five times and that each of her husbands had died mysterious and unexplained deaths. These details have never been verified. If they are true, they suggest that Eva Dugan may have been a serial killer.

The other concerned the "mysterious" Jack. It was suggested that Jack may have been real after all and that he was, in fact, Edward Hickman, a habitual criminal who went by the self-applied nickname "The Fox." Hickman matched the description of "Jack" that Eva had given to the police. He'd also been in the vicinity of Phoenix at the time of Andrew Mathis's disappearance. But Hickman would never be questioned regarding the Mathis murder. He was convicted in California of the gruesome mutilation murder of 12-year-old Marion Parker and was hanged for that crime on October 19, 1928.

Anna Carolina Jatobá

Born in São Paulo, Brazil on April 18, 2002, Isabella Nardoni entered the world in less than ideal circumstances. Her parents were a young unwed couple, both in their teens when Isabella was born. Still, they had prospects. Her father, Alexandre, was a bright young man who had just been accepted into law school; her mother, Ana, was mature for her years and determined to be a good parent despite the unexpected pregnancy. Unfortunately, she'd have to fulfill that role as a single mom. Alexandre had barely begun his university studies when Ana began to suspect that he was cheating on her. He denied this and kept up his denials for a year before Ana caught him in a lie. Then, he eventually broke down and admitted that he had been seeing someone, a fellow law student named Anna Carolina Jatobá.

The relationship between Ana and Alexandre was over. But they remained committed to doing what was best for their daughter. Isabella would remain with her mother and would also have the support of her grandparents since Ana had moved back to her parental home. Alexandre would provide whatever financial assistance he could. Later, when Isabella was around three years old, she'd start spending more time with her father. Eventually, a routine was established where Isabella spent every second weekend with her father. By then, Alexandre had married his college fling, Anna Carolina Jatobá, and the couple had two young sons together – Pietro and Cauã.

Such custody arrangements are, of course, commonplace in modern society, and usually the arrangements are cordially maintained. This case, however, was not one of those instances. Anna Jatobá was a pathologically jealous woman who hated the fact that her husband had a child by another woman. Outwardly, she appeared to treat her stepdaughter well, but there is evidence to suggest that this was not the case. Alexandre's mother once told a neighbor that she feared Jatobá might someday hurt the child. The family also took the extraordinary step of ensuring that one of them was always around if Alexandre couldn't be. They appeared terrified of leaving the little girl alone with Jatobá. As for Isabella, the normally well-behaved child would often kick up a fuss about spending time with her father. And she often arrived home from these weekends in a distressed state. Regrettably, no one appears to have delved deeper into the child's emotional state.

At around 10:30 p.m. on the evening of Saturday March 29, 2008, emergency services in São Paulo received a frantic call about a child who had fallen from the sixth floor of an apartment block. Responders rushed to the Edifício London complex where they found 5-year-old Isabella Nardoni lying in the building's front garden. The little girl was unconscious but still breathing, so the paramedics applied emergency CPR and continued their resuscitation efforts as the child was being rushed by ambulance to a nearby hospital. Unfortunately, Isabella didn't make it. Despite the best efforts of the rescuers, she died en route.

While all of this was going on, Alexandre Nardoni and Anna Jatobá had been taken in for questioning by the police. The story that they told immediately raised the suspicions of detectives. According to Nardoni, the family had arrived home from an outing at around 10:30 that evening. All three of the children had been asleep in the car, and so he'd told his wife to wait in the vehicle while he carried Isabella up to the apartment and put her to bed. He'd then returned to help his wife bring the boys upstairs. This he did, putting his daughter to bed in the guest room, turning on the bedside lamp, and then going back downstairs, locking the apartment's front door on his way out.

But the moment that Nardoni returned to the apartment with his wife and sons, he noticed something amiss. The light in the guest room was off, which was unusual because Isabella liked to sleep with it on. He then entered the room to find his daughter's bed empty. He and his wife then conducted an increasingly frantic search of the apartment but turned up no trace of Isabella. It was during that search that Alexandre noticed a hole in safety net covering the front window. Peering through the gap, he was met with the horrifying sight of his daughter's broken body, lying on the ground six floors below. He speculated that someone must have entered the apartment while he was downstairs helping his wife with the boys. The intruder most probably had dropped Isabella while trying to abduct her.

To detectives, the story sounded far-fetched. And their suspicions were raised even further when Anna Jatobá's version of events was near identical to her husband's. In their experience, there were usually inconsistencies between witness statements, especially when the individuals involved had been through such a traumatic event. Their hunch was that the couple was lying.

Obtaining a search warrant for the apartment and for Alexandre Nardoni's car, investigators soon found evidence that contradicted the story they'd been told. Droplets of Isabella's blood were found inside the vehicle and on a towel inside the apartment. There was also vomit on Nardoni's t-shirt (matched by DNA to his daughter). The shirt also delivered micro traces of nylon, which were found to be from the window screen. Similar traces were lifted from a pair of scissors found inside the apartment. As horrific as it seemed, it appeared that Alexandre Nardoni had assaulted his daughter in the car, then carried her upstairs, cut through the screen and pushed her through the gap to fall to her death.

Except that this is not what happened. The autopsy would reveal that the fall was not the cause of Isabella's death. She'd been punched repeatedly in the face and then asphyxiated before being thrown out of the window. The question was, who was responsible? Since the police were not buying the "mystery intruder" story, it could only be one of two people.

On April 18, 2008, three weeks after Isabella's death, officers of the São Paulo Civil Police arrived to take Alexandre Nardoni and Anna Jatobá into custody. Despite protesting their innocence, they were charged with murder. Their trial, which began on March 22, 2010, was one of the most sensational in Brazil's long history. An informal poll, conducted via various media outlets, suggested that an astonishing 98% of Brazilians were familiar with the details of the case.

And the proceedings would do nothing to diminish their interest, particularly the testimony of the co-accused. Both continued to deny their involvement in Isabella's death, Nardoni with frequent tears, Jatobá with haughty defiance. He claimed that his daughter had been the most precious thing in his life; she insisted that Isabella was very attached to her (something which was patently untrue). They disagreed on other things too. Nardoni claimed that he had a good relationship with his wife; she said that the relationship was fractious with frequent, and vicious, fights. This appeared to be closer to the truth.

But the real issue was whether Nardoni or Jatobá had murdered Isabella, and this question was conclusively answered by the evidence. Prosecutors believed that the assault on the little girl had begun in the car, where Jatobá had struck her several times in the face causing her to bleed from the nose and mouth. Later, the assault had continued inside the apartment. It is not certain whether Jatobá had intended killing the child. However, the pressure she applied to Isabella's throat was sufficient to make her throw up and then black out.

Then Jatobá had panicked. She'd called her husband into the room and told him that Isabella was dead. He had then concocted the quite horrific plan to throw the child from the apartment window and to blame her death on an intruder. Isabella was still alive when she was pushed through the cut in the screen but, in truth, her young life had already been taken. As the autopsy would later prove, it was the strangulation that killed her. For that, her stepmother was solely responsible.

Yet, it would be Alexandre Nardoni who received the harsher sentence. He was sent to prison for 31 years, while his wife got 26 years and 8 months, at the upper limit of punishments allowed in Brazil. The sentences were met with widespread jubilation across the country. They were of little solace to the grieving family of 5-year-old Isabella de Oliveira Nardoni.

Genene Jones

On Friday, September 17, 1982, Petti McClellan brought her eight-month-old daughter, Chelsea, to the pediatric clinic in Kerrville, Texas. Chelsea was not seriously ill, but she had a cold, and having been born prematurely, with underdeveloped lungs, her mother thought it better to be safe than sorry. The Kerrville clinic had opened just a day earlier. Chelsea McClellan was its very first patient.

While Dr. Kathleen Holland discussed Chelsea's condition with the mother, pediatric nurse, Genene Jones, took the child to another area of the clinic to play. Soon after, the nurse's cries alerted them to a problem – Chelsea had stopped breathing. Jones placed an oxygen mask over the baby's face and they rushed her to the emergency room at Sid Peterson Hospital. To everyone's relief, Chelsea recovered. It seemed that the quick-thinking Jones had saved Chelsea's life, and her grateful parents were soon singing the nurse's praises around town.

Nine months later, the McClellans had cause to bring Chelsea to the clinic again, just for a routine check-up this time. Dr. Holland prescribed two standard inoculations, but shortly after nurse Jones administered the first shot, Chelsea started having difficulty breathing. It appeared that she was having a seizure, so a frantic Mrs. McClellan told the nurse to stop. Jones ignored the instruction and gave the second injection, after which the child stopped breathing altogether.

Chelsea was rushed by ambulance to Sid Peterson Hospital, with Jones cradling the baby in her arms all the way. In the ambulance, the child's breathing stalled again and her heart stopped. All attempts to revive her failed. Chelsea McClellan was pronounced dead on arrival at Sid Peterson Hospital.

Jones herself carried the child's body downstairs to the hospital morgue, sobbing hysterically. She seemed to take the death personally, but a comment made to Dr. Holland, after they'd returned to the clinic, seemed at odds with that. Jones said: "And they said there wouldn't be any excitement when we came to Kerrville."

Dr. Holland, meanwhile, was utterly bewildered by the sudden death of a seemingly healthy child. While the grief-stricken parents prepared to bury their daughter, she requested an autopsy. The results offered scant relief. Chelsea had died of SIDS, an often-fatal breathing dysfunction in babies.

One week after the funeral of Chelsea McClellan, there was a strange incident involving Genene Jones. Petti McClellan was visiting her daughter's grave at the Garden of Memories Cemetery. As she approached, she saw Jones kneeling at the grave rocking back and forth and wailing Chelsea's name over and over. Petti asked her what she was doing, but Jones gave her a blank stare and walked off without saying a word. Petti thought the behavior peculiar, but dealing with her own grief, she let it go.

Genene Jones never knew her biological parents. Born on July 13, 1950, she was immediately adopted by Dick and Gladys Jones, a wealthy couple from San Antonio, Texas. The Joneses also adopted three other children – two older and one younger than Genene. Dick Jones was a mover and shaker, a businessman and professional gambler who operated several nightclubs. He was gregarious, extravagant and generous with his money. By all accounts, the Joneses doted on their adopted brood. Life in the household was certainly never dull.

Despite this, Genene would later describe her childhood as unhappy. She considered herself the "black sheep" of the family and said that her parents favored the other children over her. She also felt isolated and disliked at school, mainly because she was overweight, she said. Former classmates tell a different story. They say she was aggressive, untrustworthy, bossy and manipulative, a compulsive liar who often feigned illness to get attention.

When Genene was 16, her brother and closest friend, Travis, was constructing a pipe bomb in his father's workshop when it blew up in his face, killing him instantly. Genene was devastated, but her behavior at the funeral, screaming and throwing herself to the floor, seemed contrived, designed to get attention. A year later, her father was diagnosed with terminal cancer. Dick Jones died shortly after Christmas 1967. Once again Genene's response was bizarre. She insisted to her mother that she wanted to leave school and get married immediately in order to alleviate the pain.

Gladys Jones managed to dissuade Genene from the idea, but shortly after graduating high school, she did marry. Her husband was James "Jimmy" Delany, a high school dropout who enlisted in the Navy shortly after the nuptials were completed. Left on her own for long periods, Genene began indulging her voracious sexual appetite by conducting affairs with several men, some of them married. She openly boasted about these relationships and also started spreading stories about being sexually abused as a child.

Then tragedy struck the Jones family again. Genene's older brother died of cancer. In typical self-centered fashion, she developed a morbid fear that she would contract the disease herself. At the time, she was working in a beauty salon, but she soon quit that job, convinced that she would contract cancer from the hair dyes she handled. Not long after, she enrolled on a year-long course to become a vocational nurse.

Genene emerged with an LVN (Licensed Vocational Nurse) qualification and a burning passion for her knew vocation. Even though an LVN is at the bottom of the nursing totem, she began presenting herself as an expert on all things medical. She made a habit of diagnosing friends and acquaintances on the spot, whether they asked her to or not.

By this time, Genene's marriage to Jimmy Delany had failed and she had a young child to support, with another on the way. She also had her first nursing job - at San Antonio's Methodist Hospital.

By all accounts, Genene Jones was a good nurse. But from early in her medical career, there were worrying signs. After just eight months at Methodist, she was fired for making decisions in areas where she had no authority. Her next job also lasted only a few months. It seemed Jones had learned nothing from her previous problems - she was fired again, and for the same reason. Which brought her to the pediatric unit at Bexar County Medical Center. Jones would enjoy a longer tenure here - and leave a bloody imprint.

The first child to die in the care of Genene Jones did not die by her hand, but from complications after surgery to address an intestinal problem. Jones responded with an over-the-top display of grief, which her colleagues found difficult to understand. She'd hardly known the child.

But the other nurses soon learned that Jones had a desperate need for attention and that the grief was not for the dead child, but rather to garner sympathy for herself. They also realized that she wanted desperately to be needed and would go out of her way to create little dramas that required her "personal attention." Jones also carried on her habit of overstepping her authority, sometimes overriding doctor's orders to do what she believed was right for the child.

Inevitably, this led to mistakes, many of which might have constituted grounds for dismissal. But Jones had acquired an ally in head nurse Pat Belko, who often covered for her. With Belko to protect her, Jones grew increasingly arrogant, aggressive and foul-mouthed. She enjoyed bragging about her sexual exploits and took to bullying new nurses, more than one of whom resigned because of her.

But it was her attitude towards her young patients that upset her colleagues most. She liked making predictions about which baby would die next. If a child's health appeared to be failing, she would announce to the other nurses, "Tonight is the night." She'd become extremely excited by the emergency procedures in trying to save a child's life, then respond with extravagant grief when the patient died. She also seemed to enjoy calling the parents to let them know that their child had passed away.

And children did die, seven over one two-week period, many of them from conditions that should not have been fatal, most on the three-to-eleven shift, Genene Jones's shift, the shift other nurses called the "Death Shift."

In 1981, six-month-old Jose Antonio Flores was admitted with minor symptoms - fever, vomiting, and diarrhea. Under Jones's care, he suddenly began suffering seizures and went into cardiac arrest. Doctors fighting to save his life noticed internal bleeding and realized that his blood wasn't clotting. Still, they managed to stabilize him. Then Jones came back on duty at three the following day, and Jose again went into seizure and started bleeding. Early the next morning, his little heart stopped beating. An autopsy would later indicate an overdose of heparin, an anticoagulant drug.

When a three-month-old boy developed similar symptoms, a doctor confronted Jones and asked her about the heparin in his system. She angrily denied any knowledge and stormed out. Thereafter, the child recovered and no action was taken against Jones, although stricter controls were put in place over the use of the drug.

In November 1981, the head of the pediatrics ward, Dr. James Robotham, raised concerns about Genene Jones with hospital administrators. They decided that the hospital didn't need the publicity of an inquiry and told Robotham he was overreacting.

Soon after, Joshua Sawyer, 11 months old, was brought in suffering the effects of smoke inhalation. The boy was comatose, but doctors fully expected him to recover. That is until he suffered a heart attack and died. Lab tests showed a lethal amount of the drug Dilantin in his system, but no one saw fit to report this to the authorities. Again, Dr. Robotham asked that Jones be dismissed. Again he was ignored.

The next suspicious incident to occur at Bexar involved Rolando Santos, a one-month-old being treated for pneumonia. He suddenly started having seizures, went into cardiac arrest, and suffered extensive unexplained bleeding. When Jones was off for three days, Rolando's condition improved markedly. When she returned to duty, he began hemorrhaging again and suffered another heart attack. Eventually, he lapsed into a coma. Fortunately, a doctor intervened and had him removed from the pediatric unit. The little boy then made a full recovery, and the doctor who had treated him added his voice to Robotham's, calling for an inquiry. Amazingly, the hospital still refused.

It would take the death of another child before they were forced to take action. Even then, they refused an inquiry, deciding instead that all Licensed Vocational Nurses on the pediatric unit should be replaced with higher qualified Registered Nurses. This meant that Jones would no longer be able to care for children. She resigned in disgust. The hospital, no doubt, was glad to see her go.

It didn't take long for Genene Jones to find another job. In 1982, Dr. Kathleen Holland opened a pediatrics clinic in Kerrville, Texas. Dr. Holland had worked with Jones at Bexar County Hospital, had, in fact, stood up for her when the accusations were flying. Dr. Holland believed Jones to be a competent nurse who just needed a second chance. She employed Jones as her assistant and gave her the title Pediatric Clinician. It was a decision she'd soon have cause to regret.

Within its first two months of operation, seven children suffered seizures at the Kerrville clinic. Kathleen Holland seemed to see nothing unusual in this disturbing pattern, but the doctors at Sid Peterson Hospital soon became suspicious, especially as the patients always recovered after receiving treatment at the hospital.

Around the time that Chelsea McClellan died, a doctor at Sid Peterson learned about the high number of infant deaths at Bexar while Genene Jones had worked there. He brought this to the attention of a committee, and they called Dr. Holland in. They asked if she was using succinylcholine, a powerful muscle relaxant, which had been found in the blood samples of children transferred from her clinic. Dr. Holland replied that she had some, but had never used it.

Shaken by her experience, Dr. Holland returned to her office where she checked on her supply of succinylcholine. She noticed immediately that the bottles had been tampered with, the original contents extracted and replaced with saline. She confronted Jones with the evidence, but the nurse was evasive and even suggested they throw the bottle away to avoid suspicion. After Dr. Holland discovered that another bottle of succinylcholine had been ordered but was missing, she fired Jones and contacted investigators, offering her full co-operation in any inquiry.

It was already too late for her business, though. The people of Kerrville had abandoned the practice in droves, and Sid Peterson hospital had suspended her privileges. Dr. Holland may have thought that she was doing a good deed by providing Jones with a job, but the cost was her livelihood, her reputation and even her marriage, as her husband initiated divorce proceedings. As a final insult, she found evidence that Jones was planning to frame her for the murders.

Genene Jones was brought to trial for the murder of Chelsea McClellan in February 1982. She was found guilty and sentenced to 99 years in prison. In November that year, she was sentenced to an additional 60 years for injuring Rolando Santos by injecting him with an undisclosed drug.

Jones will be eligible for mandatory parole in 2017, by which time she will be 66. Although suspected in the deaths of 47 more children, she was never charged with those murders.

Adriana Vasco

At around 10:30 p.m. on the night of Saturday, November 20, 1999, a security guard was driving along the Ortega Highway, a remote road that winds through the foothills above San Juan Capistrano, California. Rounding a bend, he spotted a late model Dodge Stratus parked at the side of the road with its lights on and one of its doors hanging open. Thinking that the occupants of the vehicle might require some assistance, he pulled over to check it out.

The occupants, however, were beyond help. A man sat behind the wheel, his seatbelt still in place, blood splattering the front of his shirt and highlighting his hair with crimson. He appeared to have been shot and quite clearly wasn't breathing. The would-be rescuer then cast his eye towards the passenger side where a woman sat slumped, one leg protruding from the open door, as though she'd been trying to escape her killer when she was shot. The shootings appeared to have happened quite recently, since the engine of the vehicle was still running. The victims, though, were clearly dead and so the security guard ran back to his patrol vehicle and radioed the Sheriff's department.

Officers were soon all over the murder scene where they discovered that a total of six bullets, probably .357 or .38 caliber, had been fired into the defenseless victims. The absence of shell casings pointed to a revolver as the murder weapon. Running the plates on the Dodge, investigators quickly learned the identity of the victims. They were 57-year-old Ken Stahl and his wife Carolyn Oppy-Stahl. Further inquiries revealed that Stahl was a respected anesthesiologist from Huntington Beach, California, while Carolyn worked as an optometrist. But what were they doing out here in the middle of the night? And who had killed them? And why? Robbery could certainly be ruled out since Carolyn was still wearing her diamond-encrusted wedding ring and Ken's wallet had not been touched.

The mystery only deepened the next day, as police learned that the couple had enjoyed a romantic dinner at a Mission Viejo restaurant the previous night to celebrate Carolyn's 44th birthday. They'd left the restaurant shortly before ten. But why had they been driving east on the Ortega Highway, in the opposite direction to their Huntington Beach home? Also baffling to investigators was the reason for the killings. With robbery ruled out, the most obvious motive was revenge. Yet Ken and Carolyn appeared to have no enemies. Ken was described by friends and colleagues as mild-mannered and generous, Carolyn as outgoing and bubbly and much-loved by her patients. Both were members of First Baptist Church of Pomona, and Ken was known to carry a miniature New Testament with him at all times. They did not seem like the kind of people who might anger someone enough to commit murder. None of it made any sense.

Even at this early stage of the investigation, the police were beginning to fear that the case might go unsolved. A thorough examination of the crime scene had turned up not a single workable clue, and the remote location meant that there was no one who had seen or heard anything. But then detectives subpoenaed Ken Stahl's pager records and got what appeared to be a promising break. On the day of the murder, Stahl had received several messages from a woman named Adriana Vasco. A bit of digging revealed that Vasco had once worked as a receptionist at the hospital where Dr. Stahl was employed. She was 32 years old and an unwed mother of two. Apparently, she was also close enough to Ken Stahl to have his private pager number.

Adriana was brought in for questioning but assured the detectives that there was nothing untoward about the pager messages. She said that she'd spoken to Ken that day because she was having problems with her home computer and he "knew about these things." The officers had no reason to disbelieve her explanation. After all, initial impressions were that Stahl had been a stand-up guy.

Or had he? As detectives delved deeper, they began to uncover some startling information about the saintly Ken Stahl. The dedicated doctor, the Bible-carrying Samaritan, the loving husband, appeared to have been hiding some dirty little secrets. He was a serial philanderer who had carried on a string of affairs during his 14-year marriage to Carolyn. According to friends, Carolyn was well aware of his indiscretions and had at one stage contemplated divorce. She'd been dissuaded from doing so by Ken's mother, who had urged the couple to seek marriage counseling instead.

So if Ken Stahl was not as squeaky clean as he at first appeared, if he regularly fooled around with other women, what were the chances that he might have been sleeping with his attractive former receptionist

Adriana Vasco? The investigative team decided to bring Adriana back in for another round of questioning, and this time she admitted that she and Ken had been involved in a relationship. She insisted, however, that she'd ended the affair in 1996, after Ken refused to leave his wife. He'd told her that a divorce would damage his reputation and that he also did not want to hurt his mother, who was fond of Carolyn.

Adriana's story had again been delivered in a convincing manner, and she was allowed to leave. However, her admission that she'd been sleeping with Ken Stahl and that he'd refused to leave his wife for her, gave her motive. From this point on, she became the prime suspect, and nothing that the police uncovered over the next year would challenge that status. They learned, for example, that the affair had not ended in 1996, as Adriana had claimed. Just months before the murders, she had admitted to her supervisor that she and Ken were involved in a "long-term" relationship. At around that time, Adriana was seen wearing several items of diamond jewelry. The appearance of those items coincided with a large cash withdrawal from one of Ken Stahl's bank accounts.

But Ken was not the only man in Adriana's life at the time. She'd also been sleeping with Tony Satton, a handyman at her apartment complex. Interestingly, Satton had quit his job shortly after the double homicide, apparently to return to his native North Carolina. Further investigation revealed that his name was not Satton at all. He was Dennis Earl Godley, an ex-con with a lengthy rap sheet and outstanding fugitive warrants from two different states. Godley was known as "the Weasel" because of his uncanny ability to evade the police. Now, it appeared that he'd given them the slip again.

In October 2000, investigators again asked Adriana down to the station to answer some questions. This time, they got her to admit that Ken Stahl had come to loathe his wife and had felt trapped in the marriage. She denied, however, that Ken had ever spoken of harming Carolyn. That testimony was directly contradicted by a man named Richard Anaya, an electrician who had done work for the Stahls. He informed the police that Ken had once offered him money to kill his wife. Anaya had refused and had later decided that Stahl, who had been slightly inebriated at the time, had probably been joking with him.

But what if Stahl hadn't been joking? What if he'd looked elsewhere for a hitman? What if the hitman he found was ex-con Dennis Godley, who just happened to share a lover with him? As detectives started looking into these possibilities, a number of intriguing clues began to emerge. They learned, for example, that Adriana had been due to visit her grandmother on the day that Ken and Carolyn were murdered but had canceled at the last moment saying that she was stressed and was going to unwind by taking a drive along the Ortega Highway. That same night, Dennis Godley had attended a friend's birthday party but had left early, saying that he had another commitment. There was other evidence too, albeit circumstantial. Soon after the murders came to light, Adriana had begged her supervisor not to tell anyone about her relationship with Ken, saying that she did not want anyone to think she might be involved. And when police searched a storage unit leased by Dennis Godley, the found another connection to the crime – driver's license photographs of Ken and Carolyn Stahl.

Even with these latest pieces of the puzzle, the case was far from solid. Nonetheless, the police decided that it was time to make their move. Two days after Christmas 2000, they arrested Adriana Vasco and charged her with two counts of murder. At the same time, a warrant was issued for Dennis Godley, who remained at large.

Thirteen months had lapsed since the brutal slayings of Ken and Carolyn Stahl, thirteen months during which Adriana Vasco had no doubt believed she'd gotten away with murder. In any case, she appeared stunned by her arrest, more stunned still when investigators made clear their intentions. They had enough evidence to prove her guilty, they said, and when they did, the D.A. was going to go all out for the death penalty. Faced with that prospect, Adriana almost immediately cracked and started talking. The story she had to tell was one of the most twisted the investigators had ever heard.

According to Adriana's version of events, the plot had been set in motion after Ken had started talking about having his wife "knocked off." He could have divorced Carolyn and been no worse off financially since there was a pre-nuptial agreement in place. However, to Ken, it was about more than just money. Divorce would have painted him as a failure in the eyes of his family, and he wasn't prepared to countenance that. He'd rather have Carolyn killed. He was prepared to pay $30,000 for the hit.

A short while later, Adriana was discussing Ken's predicament with her other lover Dennis Godley. In her self-serving retelling of events, Adriana claimed that she was both drunk and under the influence of drugs at the time and that she'd only been joking when she'd suggested that Dennis might be interested in taking the job. Dennis, however, had taken her seriously and had told her to set up a meeting with Ken. When Adriana had then tried to back out, he'd threatened to hurt her and her children.

Thus was the murder plot set in motion. A meeting was set up between the men with Adriana acting as go-between. Later, Ken had handed her an envelope stuffed with cash which she'd passed on to Dennis. Thereafter, the men had spoken several times on the phone to hash out the details. Eventually, it was decided that Ken would take his wife to a surprise birthday dinner and would then persuade her to take a moonlight drive on the Ortega highway. He'd pull the car over at a prescribed spot, ostensibly to admire the lights of San Juan Capistrano, in the valley below. That was when Godley would emerge from the shadows to gun Carolyn down. Adriana claimed that she tried several times to dissuade Dennis from carrying out the hit but that he'd refused and warned her not to interfere.

On the night of the murders, Adriana picked Dennis up and drove to a gas station on the Ortega Highway, where they waited for Carolyn's silver Dodge Stratus to appear. When it did, Adriana followed, keeping a safe distance until she saw the Stratus pull over. She then passed and did a U-turn, stopping on the blacktop. She remained in the vehicle, while Dennis got out and approached the other car. Moments later, she heard gunshots and Carolyn's screams. Dennis then returned to the vehicle and reloaded. When she asked what he was doing, he said that Carolyn was still alive. He then walked back to the Stratus and fired several more shots. It was only when they were driving away that Dennis told her that he'd shot Ken too. He said that he'd done it because he didn't want to leave any witnesses behind. Adriana suspected that his real reason was that he was jealous of her relationship with Ken.

Adriana was still telling that same convoluted story when she appeared before the courts in January 2003. However, the jury found her no more believable than the police had and found her guilty of the first-degree murder of Carolyn Oppy-Stahl and the second-degree murder of Ken Stahl. She was sentenced to life in prison without parole. Dennis Godley had meanwhile been captured in North Carolina and was extradited to California to face two counts of murder. He pleaded guilty and received the same sentence as his one-time lover.

Tracy Garrison

"Frankly, you scare me to death. You are a frightening, frightening individual." These were the words spoken by California Superior Court Judge Christian Thierbach to the murder defendant he had just sentenced to life in prison without parole. The defendant looked right back at him, showing no sign of emotion. The petite brunette was contemplating the weight of the sentence the judge had just handed down to her. When you are just 22 years old, a life sentence is an awfully long time.

The series of events that had landed Tracy Garrison in the dock, charged with a murder, had begun a decade earlier when she was 12 years old. That was when she'd first tried alcohol, decided that the effects were to her liking, and then quickly graduated to much harder drugs. By her mid-teens, she was a hardcore meth user who mainlined heroin when she could get her hands on it, and smoked marijuana several times a day. At 22, she had a lover who could match her hit for hit. Joshua Blaine Wahlert was a dangerous man, a former Hell's Angel who smoked and spiked whatever he could get his hands on, usually meth or heroin. He was also a hardcore drinker and violent with it. Tracy called him Clyde. He called her Bonnie.

Of course, every junkie needs a dealer, and in the case of Wahlert and Garrison, that role was filled by 39-year-old Temecula, California native, Michael Willison. Willison ran a legitimate and successful house painting business, but his real money was made dealing meth. He also enjoyed helping himself to the merchandise on occasion and using his wares to barter for sex. One of those who regularly traded him was Tracy Garrison. In fact, Tracy shacked up with Willison every time she and her old man had a fight and he kicked her out of his Hemet, California, trailer. Those fights were frequent, but Tracy would always return within a few days. Mike was fun but he wasn't 'Clyde.' She knew where her heart lay.

We can't say for certain when (or why) Tracy Garrison first hatched the murder plot that would ultimately see her surrender her freedom, only that it was she who hatched it and not Josh Wahlert. Despite Wahlert's obvious physical advantage over her, it was Tracy who called the shots, she who carried the vindictive streak. Convincing the ex-biker was easy, in any case. He already had a seething hatred towards Michael Willison because of the time Tracy had spent with him. When she suggested killing the drug dealer, Wahlert barely flinched.

The plan that the would-be modern-day Bonnie and Clyde concocted was hardly original. They were going to abduct Willison from his home, drive him to a remote location and shoot him dead. Then they were going to raid his house for cash, valuables, and drugs. Finally, they were going to take Willison's truck and drive to Las Vegas where they planned to get married. And they were hardly discreet about this hare-brained scheme. They discussed it with another junkie, Jon Ramirez, who was an associate of theirs and also a friend of their intended victim. Had Ramirez warned Willison of the plot against him, Willison might have taken steps to avoid his fate. But Ramirez did not warn his friend. He'd later claim that he thought Wahlert and Garrison were just blowing smoke. He'd heard more than his fair share of drugged-out talk in the past, he said. Usually, it came to nothing.

But in this case, it seems that the talk was not idle, the intent quite sincere. On January 14, 2001, Wahlert burst into Willison's home waving a gun, Garrison right behind him. Willison had just finished taking what would turn out to be his last ever hit on a meth pipe when Wahlert pointed the weapon at him and warned him not to 'start any shit' if he wanted to live. Ramirez, who was also present, sat buzzing on his host's crank and said nothing. He made no effort to intervene when Willison was gagged and had his hands and mouth bound with duct tape. He did nothing as Willison was dragged from the house. Later, he'd tell police that Willison had begged Wahlert and Garrison not to hurt him, saying that he wanted to be around to see his kids grow up.

Those pleas would fall on deaf ears. Willison was manhandled into his own truck and driven to a remote location in Riverside County. There he was pistol-whipped into submission and then shot twice. Still not content with the damage he'd inflicted, Wahlert then pulled a knife and plunged it repeatedly into his helpless victim. Wahlert and Garrison then drove away from the scene, leaving Willison to bleed out in the brush. When they returned, less than an hour later, they found that their intended victim was not yet dead. Willison had been able to pull himself some six feet through the dirt, leaving behind a trail of blood. But now his strength was exhausted. Wahlert finished him off with a flurry of knife thrusts to the back that perforated every major organ.

In the aftermath of the killing, Wahlert and Garrison again displayed a startling lack of caution regarding their crime. First they tracked down Ramirez and gave him Willison's ring and a necklace as compensation for "having to see what went down." Then Garrison boasted to a friend about the killing, and Wahlert told a different friend, "I tried to rob the guy, but things got out of hand so I shot him, stabbed him and split."

He also continued driving Willison's truck and tried, on several occasions, to use his credit cards. In one such incident, he sped away from a gas station when he thought that the attendant was going to call the police over the rejected transaction.

Yet despite their stupidity, Wahlert and Garrison might still have gotten away with murder had Michael Willison's body not been found. Unfortunately for them, the spot they had chosen was not as isolated as they had believed. Within days of the murder, a jogger stumbled upon the desecrated corpse and reported it to the police, who immediately secured the scene and started combing for clues. This case, however, would not be solved by brilliant detective work but by the sheer ineptitude of the perpetrators.

Riverside County detectives had only just begun their investigation when Josh Wahlert all but walked himself into their police custody. Arrested on January 20 for brandishing a firearm in public, a drugged-up Wahlert told police officers, "I'm looking at 60 years minimum. You haven't found out the half of it yet."

The case fell together quite quickly after that. Wahlert was driving a dead man's truck, which had several smears of blood inside, later proven to be from the victim; he had that victim's credit cards tucked into his wallet along with an uncashed payroll check; he had Willison's Social Security card. Not that Wahlert was in the mood to deny anything. He quickly confessed under interrogation, saying that Tracy Garrison had been present but had not participated in any way. Garrison was tracked down and placed under arrest anyway. She was far less forthcoming than her partner in crime, claiming that she'd remained in the truck the whole time and had done nothing to harm

Willison. However, she'd later implicate herself during a telephone conversation with Wahlert which was recorded by police.

Tracy Garrison and Joshua Wahlert were tried separately for the murder of Michael Willison. At Wahlert's trial, the defense contended that Garrison had used Wahlert's jealousy towards Willison to manipulate him into committing murder. Wahlert repeated that allegation on the stand, saying that Garrison had used him to "get the dude done." He also changed his tune about Garrison's involvement in the actual killing, saying that she had helped subdue Willison and had bound his wrists and taped over his mouth while Wahlert held a gun on him. Wahlert was ultimately found guilty and sent to prison for life without parole. He thanked the judge for the sentence, saying, "I don't deserve to be a free man."

Tracy Garrison's defense followed a somewhat different narrative to that of Joshua Wahlert. According to her attorney, she was as much a victim of this crime as Michael Willison. She'd only gone along with the plan because Wahlert had threatened to kill her if she did not. As a reluctant accomplice, she did not deserve a custodial sentence. Justice would be best served if she were to be acquitted outright or, at worst, given probation.

Unfortunately for Garrison, there was testimony to refute her version of events. Jon Ramirez had been present at the time of the abduction and said that Tracy appeared to be a willing participant. Several other witnesses testified that she had boasted about the murder and the role she had played in it. In the end, it was a simple matter for the jurors. They took just three hours to find Tracy Garrison guilty of first-degree murder. Like her one-time lover, she was sentenced to life without parole. Unlike him, she offered no words of remorse.

Deanna Laney

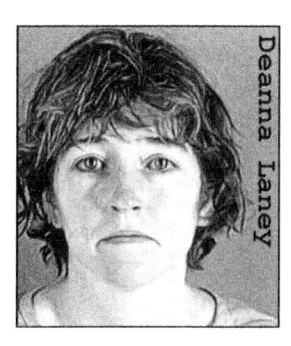

To anyone looking from the outside in, the Laney family of New Chapel Hill, Texas, appeared the personification of domestic harmony. Keith and Deanna doted on their three sons, Joshua, 8, Luke, 6, and baby Aaron who was just 14 months old. The family was deeply religious and regularly attended the Assembly of God church in New Chapel Hill. Deanna, a stay-at-home mom, even decided to homeschool her children, stating that she did not want them exposed to the "evil teachings" that students were exposed to at secular schools.

In this case, however, evil was lurking much closer to home, and it came in the unlikeliest of forms. Deana's religious fanaticism was leading her down some dark roads. Recently, she'd begun to express a kinship with Andrea Yates, the Texas housewife who had drowned her five children in a bathtub in 2001, claiming that God had instructed her to do so. Laney had begun to believe that Yates's brutal act had earned her favor with God and that she would be by His side when He returned to call the righteous to salvation. In the spring of 2003, Laney began to believe that she, too, had been called to greatness.

It started with a dream in which Laney saw her fourteen-month-old son, Aaron, holding a spear. She wasn't sure what this meant exactly, but one thing was undeniable to her. The dream was a message from God. Desperate to understand its meaning, she picked up her Bible and found herself drawn to passages in which God had demanded human sacrifice. One passage that particularly attracted her attention was Genesis 22:1-18, the well-known story of Abraham and Isaac. *"Take your son, your only son – yes, Isaac, whom you love so much – and go to the land of Moriah. Sacrifice him there as a burnt offering on one of the mountains, which I will point out to you."*

That order, of course, had been a ruse. God had only been testing Abraham and had ultimately spared Isaac's life. So perhaps that is what this was. Perhaps God was putting her faith to the test. If that was the case, she would not be found wanting.

Over the days that followed, several more signs appeared. It also became clear to Laney that her situation did not bear comparison with that of the biblical Abraham. Unlike him, she would not be spared the duty of murdering her children. Her lot was more aligned with her sister in faith, Andrea Yates. She would not be relieved of her burden. God had even indicated to her the possible methods by which she might commit the atrocities. The spear in her dream suggested stabbing. In another "revelation," Aaron had handed her a small rock. That indicated stoning. Then she caught the toddler squeezing a small frog and decided that this, too, was a sign. God had given her a third option – strangulation. Thus was the goodness of the Lord. Of the three methods, she decided that stoning was probably the most humane.

But still Laney demurred, instead directing prayers towards the heavens, begging to be relieved of her duty. The answer she got back was emphatic. She would have to go through with it, acting in faith and trusting that God would use the deaths of her sons for some greater purpose. Knowing that it was pointless to resist, she decided that she would obey the command she'd been given. God had never led her wrong before.

At around midnight on May 9, 2003, Mothers' Day, Deanna Laney rose from her marital bed. Leaving her husband quietly snoring, she walked the darkened corridor and entered the room of her infant son Aaron. The little boy was sound asleep as she reached under his bed and retrieved the dinner plate sized boulder that she'd hidden there earlier in the day. Hefting the rock, she brought it to shoulder height and then crashed it down onto the head of the sleeping child. It was not a clean strike. Aaron was hurt but not killed. He started wailing, bringing his father running from the bedroom. Laney, with her back to her husband and shielding Aaron from view, told him that the 14-month-old had just woken from a bad dream. She told Keith to go back to bed, and he complied. As soon as he walked away, she placed a pillow over the toddler's head and suffocated him.

Keith's near intervention had been a close call, but Laney was now determined that nothing would stand in the way of her duty. Leaving Aaron's room, she walked to the bedroom of 6-year-old Luke, roused him from sleep and told him to follow her out into the garden. There, she brutally bludgeoned him to death with the rock. By now spattered with blood but acting with cold-minded determination, Laney dragged the boy's body out of sight before bringing her third son, 8-year-old Joshua, out into the yard and killing him, too. Then she walked calmly back into the house and dialed 911. "I killed my boys," she told the stunned dispatcher.

Police officers and paramedics were soon rushing to the scene, a modest bungalow on a quiet suburban street. There they found Laney, standing in a blood-soaked nightdress and her husband, still groggy from sleep, first bewildered and then horrified by what had happened. Luke and Joshua were dead, their bodies lying side by side in the garden with a large stone placed on each of their chests. Aaron, the baby, had miraculously survived. He was rushed to hospital where doctors would ultimately save his life. However, he'd suffered brain damage and would be vision-impaired and physically disabled for the rest of his life.

Laney was taken into custody. But it was clear from the start that this was no ordinary case. Despite having just clubbed two of her sons to death; despite having critically injured her 14-month-old baby, she was entirely calm, serene even. There were no tears, no regrets. A smile played across her lips as she told detectives that she had done what God had asked of her. "His will be done," was her oft-repeated refrain. She also insisted that her children were not dead, that they were merely awaiting the resurrection.

Six days later, when she was first interviewed by a psychiatrist, Laney's demeanor had not changed and neither had her story. "I am God's loyal servant," she said. "He will reveal His power and my children will be raised up. They will become alive again." Her only regret, she said, was that she had not killed all three of her boys, as God had instructed. Aaron had lived. As penance for this, she refused to drink water except that which she could lap from the toilet bowl in her cell.

Deanna Laney went on trial in early 2004. Because of her quite obvious psychosis, the defense was presented with a clear strategy – to plead her not guilty by reason of insanity. To this extent, they produced a couple of psychiatrists who testified that Laney had been delusional and psychotic at the time of the murders and could not appreciate that what she was doing was wrong. The prosecution, of course, produced its own experts. But in a surprising twist, they agreed with the defense's assessment of Laney's mental state. Court-appointed psychiatrist, Dr. William Reed, went one step further. He described Deanna Laney as "crazy."

With all of the experts apparently in agreement as to the defendant's state of mind, it was hardly surprising that the jury acquitted Deanna Laney of murder on April 3, 2004. Laney was then ordered to be detained at a maximum security mental hospital, with prosecutors stating their belief that she would never be released.

That prediction, however, would prove wide of the mark. Laney was originally held at the maximum security Vernon State Hospital but was transferred within months to Kerrville State Hospital, a non-secure inpatient facility. Within a year, she was receiving regular unsupervised furloughs, using these to visit her parents, to go shopping, and to enjoy restaurant meals. Prosecutors only got to hear of this in 2007 and immediately filed a petition which put a stop to these privileges.

But whatever inconvenience Laney suffered as a result, it was short-lived. In 2012, doctors at Kerrville decided that she was no longer mentally ill and authorized her release. This was ratified by a judge, and on May 24, Deanna Laney walked free. The brutal murders of her sons had cost her just nine years of incarceration.

For more True Crime books by Robert Keller please visit
http://bit.ly/kellerbooks

Printed in Great Britain
by Amazon